Table of Contents

Section One: Core Skills

Section Two: Gig Survival

Section Three: Specialized Skills

Appendix

Acknowledgments

I'd like to thank everyone now and formerly at BASS PLAYER and Miller Freeman who gave me the opportunity to write and helped me do my job the best I can: Jim Roberts, Richard Johnston, Karl Coryat, Vicki Hartung, Greg Isola, Greg Olwell, Bill Leigh, Scott Malandrone, Brian Courtney, Paul Haggard, and Pat Cameron. Thanks to Matt Kelsey at Backbeat Books for putting it together. Thanks to the Keisel family, Dave Flores and everyone at Carvin, Larry and Pam Fishman at Fishman Transducers, and Richard Cocco and Bob Archigian at La Bella Strings for their wonderful support and friendship. Thanks to John Cerullo and Jeff Schroedl at Hal Leonard for making my first five books part of the Hal Leonard catalog. Thanks to my family: Sonia, Irving, LeeEllen, and Aimee Friedland, and David Taylor. Thanks to Dr. Linda Ostrander at Cambridge College for "walking" with me through the process of creating my Masters thesis, which eventually became my first book. Thanks to all of my many students over the years who have acted as (willing) test subjects for much of this book's material—I've learned as much from you as I hope you have from me. Finally, thanks to all my teachers through the years—Rudolph Blitzer, Marvin Topolsky, Joe Bongiorno, Rich Appleman, Whit Browne, Bruce Gertz, and Glen Moore—and all the many talented bassists that are my heroes, my colleagues, and my friends, for showing me how great it is to be a bass player.

The Working Bassist's Tool Kit

The Art & Craft of Successful Bass Playing

By Ed Friedland

Backbeat
Books

San Francisco

Published by Backbeat Books
600 Harrison Street
San Francisco, CA 94107
www.backbeatbooks.com
Email: books@musicplayer.com
An imprint of the Music Player Network
United Entertainment Media, Inc.

Distributed to the book trade in the U.S. and Canada by
Publisher's Group West, 1700 Fourth Street, Berkeley, CA 94710

Distributed to the music trade in the U.S. and Canada by
Hal Leonard Publishing, P.O. Box 13819, Milwaukee, WI 53213

Front Cover Design: Paul Haggard
Back Cover Design and Cover Composition: Greene Design
Text Design and Composition: Greene Design

Library of Congress Cataloging-in-Publication Data

Friedland, Ed.
    The working bassist's tool kit : the art and craft of successful bass playing
    / by Ed Friedland.
        p.cm
    ISBN 0-87930-615-7 (alk. paper)
    1. Bass guitar--Instruction and study. I. Title.

MT599.B4 F97 2000
787.87'193--dc21

                                                                00-056057

        04 05   5 4 3

About the Author

A graduate of New York City's High School of Music and Art, Ed Friedland has taught at Berklee College of Music, Boston College, Arizona State University, and Milton Academy. He is a contributing editor for BASS PLAYER and is the author of *Building Walking Bass Lines, Expanding Walking Bass Lines, Jazz Bass, Bass Improvisation*, and *Reggae Bass* for Hal Leonard. He has an M.Ed. from Cambridge College, Cambridge, Massachusetts.

His performance credits include work with Larry Coryell, Michal Urbaniak, Ursula Dudziak, Robben Ford, Sal Nistico, Illinois Jacquette, Jimmy Maxwell, Jimmy McPartland, Junior Cook, Eddie Daniels, George Garzone, Rebecca Parris, Mike Metheny, Paul Horn, Gray Sargent, John Stowell, Mark Elf, Joshua Breakstone, Randy Johnston, Kitty Margolis, Johnny Adams, Linda Hopkins, Robert Jr. Lockwood, Mighty Sam McClain, Martha & the Vandellas, the Marvellettes, the Drifters, the Platters, Brook Benton, Georgie Jessel, Tiny Tim, Jack Carter, Lawrence Hilton Jacobs, Demond Wilson, Al Martino, Tony Martin, Suzanne Sommers, Vic Damone, Dianne Carroll, the New Christy Minstrels, and Anna Maria Alberghetti. He has performed in the Boston and Tokyo productions of *Little Shop of Horrors*, the Boston productions of *Nite Club Confidential* and *A Closer Walk with Patsy Cline*, the Opera Company of Boston's production of Leonard Bernstein's *Mass*, and the Arizona Theater Company's production of Gershwin's *Fascinating Rhythm*. Ed's also brought his bass skills to numerous recording sessions and countless one-nighters.

Foreword

I started working as a professional bassist in 1978. In my career I've learned two of the best things about being a bass player are, one, never having to worry what you're going to do on Saturday night and, two, being able to choose from a wide variety of gigs. Throughout the years I've played in theater orchestras, big bands, symphonies, rock bands, R&B and blues bands, straightahead jazz and fusion groups, country and country-Western bands, Cajun and zydeco bands, and Brazilian bands. I've backed up oldies acts and Vegas acts and played studio dates of all types; toured Europe, South America, Canada, and the United States; and played more weddings than any one man should be allowed to.

While every situation was different, my employers always depended on me to perform the basic duties expected from a professional bassist. And as I became more involved in bass education, I found that beyond learning the specifics of a particular style, what bassists need to learn are fundamental skills that can be transferred to all styles. These skills include keeping time, creating a groove, playing lines that indicate a chord progression, following a chord chart, reading music, being able to anticipate chord movements and play songs by ear, and knowing how to assess a situation and provide what is needed.

When BASS PLAYER first showed up in 1989, I was thrilled to see a magazine just for us low-enders, and I saw an opportunity to bring important practical information to a large number of players. So I was delighted when founding Editor Jim Roberts accepted my "Metronome as Guru" story for the September 1992 issue.

After BP printed my first piece, I was unstoppable. I pitched many ideas for articles to help readers learn skills and hone their strengths, and Jim never said no. Over the years my catalog of articles kept growing. When Jim became Miller Freeman's Music Group Publisher, BP's new Editor, Karl Coryat, asked me to write a monthly beginners column—which I called "The Right Foot"—and he then gave me an official title, Contributing Editor. Though I'm still waiting for my key to the executive washroom, I'm still officially part of the BASS PLAYER team. I'm extremely proud of that association, and I'm grateful to have the continuing opportunity to keep BP the world's best magazine for bassists.

Current Editor Richard Johnston has allowed me to broaden my scope at BASS PLAYER and develop into something of a real journalist. I've had the opportunity to interview some great unsung players, some of my personal heroes, and some bass legends. Hey, I love this job!

When I looked back on my many instructional articles, I realized it was time for a BASS PLAYER book for players "in the trenches." Free of the magazine format's space constraints, I have expanded on my original ideas and provided audio examples to help the reader get the most out of the learning process.

About This Book

The purpose of this book is to teach bassists the essential skills a professional player needs. If you're already an experienced pro, *The Working Bassist's Tool Kit* provides ways to sharpen your skills and perhaps develop new ones. If you're a new player looking to make a living in music, you'll find what you need to get started.

The Working Bassist's Tool Kit is organized in three sections. Section One, Core Skills, addresses the most crucial abilities you need to be a professional player: playing in time and grooving, reading chord charts, and hearing pitches and chord changes. Section Two, Gig Survival, goes beyond technical ability to explore the many other concrete and conceptual skills you need to tackle any kind of gig. Section Three, Specialized Skills, gives you a competitive edge by exploring techniques to make you stand out as a player.

The amount of information in this book is vast and varied and will require dedication and patience to learn. It has taken me more than 22 years of gigging to amass this knowledge, so I don't expect you to master it in six months or even a year. And the more real-life experience you get, the more relevant the information will become. This has been true for me—I'm still learning new things every time I play. When you reach the top of one mountain, you can clearly see the other mountains that lie ahead.

Using the CD

The CD with this book is designed to maximize the material's educational value. In general, the tracks are presented in the split-mix format. The bass is isolated in the right channel, and the rest of the accompaniment is in the left. This lets you hear the bass example in context and then turn off the accompaniment so you can take over the job. In some cases (the ear training examples, for instance) the split mix is not needed. In the book, examples that appear on the CD are designated by a number within a diamond. The number corresponds to the example's CD track number.

I produced all of the CD tracks at home using OpCode Vision sequencing software, a variety of synthesizer gear, some guitars, a few basses, and a Roland VS-880 Digital Studio Workstation.

Section
One

Core Skills

Chapter 1

Keeping Time

This chapter combines material from my three major BASS PLAYER articles on time-keeping and groove playing: "The Metronome as Guru" (April 1993), "Grooving on the Grid" (July 1995), and "Get Great Time" (April 1999).

Timekeeping skills are at the core of all good bass playing. However, a list of essential bass functions looks like this:

1. Outline the root motion

2. Keep track of the form

3. Create lines that support the music

4. Balance creativity with functionality

5. Have sufficient technical skills to meet the music's demands

6. Play with a sound that enhances the music

Notice how I didn't say anything about time? That's because without time and groove, nothing else matters! Even if you can perform all of those listed functions, if you can't keep time you won't get gigs. That means being able to play one note after the other without speeding up or slowing down. And the better your time, the more likely other musicians will want to work with you.

Nonetheless, timekeeping is often overlooked by bassists in pursuit of other pleasures. Having god-like technical facility, the coolest equipment, and the right clothes, hair, attitude, and promo shot are all ways to convince yourself you have it together. We've all seen such deluded individuals trying to get gigs, trying to keep gigs they've shmoozed their way into, getting fired from gigs they were ill prepared for, and convincing themselves they're too good for the scene and need to be in a bigger town to really make it. But you can be spared these illusions. Start by accepting the fact that your timekeeping skills need to be developed and continually maintained. All the top players in the world do it—why not you?

Making the Most of Your Metronome

One of the best ways to develop your time sense is consistent, focused practice with a metronome. Since you can trust an electronic metronome not to speed up or slow down, it's the perfect tool for measuring your accuracy. But will using a metronome turn you into a bass robot, rigidly adhering to the beat and forsaking any human feeling or groove? Don't worry—as soon as you turn off the click you're on your own.

Your sense of time comes from an internal clock that runs on a rechargeable battery. When you first use a rechargeable battery, you have to charge it for a long time. Likewise, when you are first developing your internal clock, you need to "charge" it by working hard with a metronome. Once your sense of time is up and running, you can stay fully charged by regularly tapping into the source—the ever-swirling continuum of time that surrounds us. Eventually, your internal clock will keep going when you shut off your metronome.

Your internal clock can become very accurate, but it will never be as strict as a machine. Add a drummer, a guitarist or two, a keyboard player, and a singer, and suddenly you have five different time feels trying to connect. That's when you'll appreciate the hours spent with the metronome—those other players rely on you to be *their* metronome. Also, a large amount of studio work and some live gigs involve playing to a click track or sequenced keyboards, and your metronome practice will keep you from wasting session time and losing the beat in front of an audience.

These days many bassists practice by playing along with complicated drum-machine patterns. While this approach can be interesting and fun, it's not the best way to produce rhythmic self-sufficiency. Drum machines are great for working out songs, but for strictly developing your time, they make your work a little too easy—and they will not make you as strong as you need to be to survive in the highly competitive gig world. There are many bass players who can furiously spew endless funk triplets and tapped harmonics, but the ones who do it *in time* are the ones who get the gig.

Daily Rituals. The following "rituals" will help you get comfortable with the metronome, with the goal of gradually decreasing your reliance on it so you can use it merely as a reinforcement. Practice these exercises daily with patient and diligence, and you'll walk into your gigs a timekeeping powerhouse!

Ex. 1 is simple to grasp yet poses a big challenge. Play a major scale with the metronome beating two clicks per written note. Start at a medium tempo, 70–80 BPM. Let the click become part of the scale. Practice at this tempo awhile to get comfortable, and then slow down to 40 BPM. After playing the exercise slowly, crank the metronome to top speed (208–240 BPM). Since you're playing half-notes, it's actually a medium tempo—the trick is to stay relaxed with the double-time click hammering away at you. Stay calm by counting slower. For each four clicks, count one beat and play half-notes, so you're counting half as slowly as you are playing.

Ex. 1

For Ex. 2 play the scale with the metronome clicking quarter-notes. Focus on nailing each note to the click. Try to feel the missing click from the previous exercise. Don't just attempt to play to the click—bring it inside you and make it a part of the scale.

Ex. 2

Ex. 3 puts the metronome click on every other note, beats *one* and *three*. Find a manageable tempo and focus on keeping the rhythm consistent. Once you have a feel for this, do the exercise at extreme slow and fast tempo ranges.

Ex. 3

Ex. 4 is another time-honored metronome method, putting the click on beats *two* and *four* like a backbeat (in pop music usually played on the snare drum, in jazz with the hi-hat). With the click no longer on the downbeat, you're responsible for laying down the *one*. This is the essence of a bass player's job. To get in the groove with this exercise, slap your hand on your knee with the click. When your hand is in the air, start counting on beat *one* so your slap falls on *two* and *four*. When you're comfortable with this, take familiar bass lines and practice them with the *two* and *four* click. Listen for how the click fits into the rhythmic pattern. Practice your walking lines, slap licks, and band lines this way. You'll find that the groove is all about *two* and *four* placement.

Ex. 4

Slow and Slower. For the next series of rituals, slow down the metronome all the way. Now it will click once every four notes. Even at 40 BPM, these exercises may be a little fast. If you have a drum machine you may be able to slow down the tempo even more, although it becomes even harder to stay with the click at tempos below 40. Either way, this one is a challenge.

Examples 5a–5d remove the click even further from the equation—there's only one click for every four notes played. Ex. 5a is the easiest; feeling the click on the downbeat is very natural.

For Ex. 5b start counting on the click, but count this way: <u>*two*</u>, *three, four, one,* <u>*two*</u>, *three, four, one,* <u>*two*</u>, *three, four,* etc. Once you get comfortable with the count, shift the count's accent to one, keeping the click on two. When you can feel beat one as the downbeat, start playing. Focus on the groove it creates.

Ex. 5c is a half-time backbeat, which also feels natural. Start your count like this: <u>*three*</u>, *four, one, two,* <u>*three*</u>, *four, one, two,* etc. Then, as before, shift the accent to one.

Ex. 5d is tricky but not impossible. Count <u>*four*</u>, *one, two, three,* <u>*four*</u>, *one, two, three,* etc., and then shift the accent to one. You can also try starting your count right after the click: *click, one, two, three, four, one, two, three,* etc.

Ex. 5a–d

Each of these exercises has a distinctive feel. The more difficult ones will help you focus on the beat wherever it lies—odd beat placements are common in funk, fusion, progressive rock, jazz, and non-Western music. These rituals will help you to solidify your concentration on the beat.

High and Higher. The following rituals are very advanced. They require a fairly high level of technical skill because they are fast—even at 40 BPM. Set the click to play once every other bar, or eight notes per click. Some of the exercises are difficult to count and feel, so be patient and don't give up. Your new sense of confidence in your time will be ample reward.

For Examples 6a–6d count this way: *one, two, three, four, two, two, three, four.* This will help you keep track of which bar you're in. Ex. 6a is relatively easy; most people practice scales with the click on one. For Ex. 6b start your count on the click, this way: *two, three, four, two, two, three, four.* Then shift the accent to the one of the first bar: *one, two, three, four, two, two, three, four.* Once you can feel one as the downbeat, start playing.

For Ex. 6c start counting *three, four, two, two, three, four.* Then shift the accent to the *one* of the first bar. Start playing when you feel it. You know what to do for Ex. 6d.

Ex. 6a–d

Working with the metronome is a very deep pursuit, and you can take it as far as you can imagine. It's important to stay focused on being accurate, because all your work will be meaningless if you're not. Don't settle for good enough—do it for real and try to bring out the rhythm inside you. You will sometimes need to screen out rhythmic interference and focus on your own internal time; all it takes is one person in a band with bad time (pray it isn't the drummer!) to make your job ten times harder. That's when you'll be glad you spent your time with the metronome.

Examples 7a–7d are extremely challenging. They will take a lot of practice and perseverance to get comfortable with. Stay focused on the downbeat and let the click simply reinforce the time.

Ex. 7a is a welcome break: a half-time backbeat. No problem! This is good for developing a 16th-note funk groove.

Try Ex. 7b. Now the click is getting so far away from the downbeat that it's easier to begin counting from the other bar. Concentrate on feeling the notes' pulse. Then, on the click, count three beats and start on one: *one, two, three, one, two, three, four, two, two, three, four*. This makes it easier to get going.

Use the same method for Ex. 7c. Feel the pulse. Then, starting on the click, count two notes: *one, two, one, two, three, four, two, two, three, four*.

To count off Ex. 7d, use the click as a pickup to the downbeat: *click, one, two, three, four, two, two, three, four*.

Ex. 7a-d

Time and space. Now that you've gone through the complete set of metronome rituals using a major scale, let's translate the idea into a more practical application. Ex. 8 is a syncopated R&B line with plenty of space. Listen carefully to how the metronome fits into the gaps. Once you relax and figure out where the click belongs, you'll be amazed how simple this kind of grooving can be. Ex. 9 is the syncopated R&B groove again, this time twice as fast and with less click to guide you. Concentrate on feeling the space between the notes, paying attention to how the downbeat click lines up with the first two eighth-notes. Ex. 10 is a bit trickier to keep grooving with the click only on *two*, but it is possible. Now you're starting to see how important your time responsibility is. Ex. 11 puts the click on beat three. Finally, we use the click on beat 4 with the R&B line (Ex. 12).

If you accept the challenge and spend a lot of time with these exercises, your pulse and groove will improve, and things you can already play will sound better. Once you've locked in, everything becomes easier and you'll no longer have to struggle to make the bass line fit—it just will naturally.

Time vs. Groove

Time and groove are closely linked, but in many ways they're two different things. There is also actual time and perceived time. A minute is 60 seconds, but a

minute of eating a great meal seems much shorter than a minute
of filling out a tax form. Understanding this helps you understand
groove. It's also important to remember good time does not ensure
a groove. Many of the great recordings have an incredible groove,
yet they are not perfectly in time. But who's going to complain
that James Brown's band rushes when they play that *D9* arpeggio

in "I Got You (I Feel Good)"? Not me—it grooves! The Rolling Stones? Jimmy Reed? Professor Longhair? You can't set your watch by these guys, but they make people move.

The next step toward groovedom is to take the metronome lessons and bring them inside yourself. You create a groove when you internalize a tune's tempo and rhythm, filter it through your groove machine (you and the bass) and connect it to the rest of the band.

How do you get the groove inside you? Your body has to get into the act. Take a walk someplace where you won't have to deal with obstructions or varying terrain. Pick a relaxed speed and assign one foot to beats *one* and *three*, the other to *two* and *four*. Now start singing a tune or bass line to yourself. Keep it up awhile and see how your body reacts. Then imagine the Count Basie band kicking into the shout chorus of "April in Paris," Bernard Odum and Clyde Stubblefield greasing their way through James Brown's "I Got the Feelin'," and Rocco Prestia and Dave Garibaldi locking into "What Is Hip?" All strong grooves, all completely different.

Another method: Turn on your metronome and count quarter-notes around 40 BPM. Stand up with your bass and stomp your right heel on *one* and *three* and the left on *two* and *four*. Gradually start to shift your body weight by alternating from one heel to the other. Once you feel locked into the beat, play something familiar. Pay attention to the click and how your body reacts to the groove, and see how much you can move with the beat. You may notice some resistance at first—stay relaxed, close your eyes, listen, feel, play.

Dance! While some of us became musicians so we could play at the prom instead of having to dance there, your groove can benefit greatly from learning to shake your thang. If you are uncomfortable dancing in public, do it at home when there's no one around. Put on your favorite groove CD and let it go! It doesn't matter what you look like—no one's watching (we hope). Start with the basic pulse, then see if you can incorporate some of the rhythmic punches, fills, cymbal crashes, and stops—anything that makes your movements one with the tune.

After you've cooled down, it's time to sing. When you're done screaming about how you *can't* sing, take a few deep breaths and relax. We're talking about something more like rhythmic scatting than actual singing—no pitch required. If you can hear a rhythm, you can sing it. Have a friend sing a rhythm to you. How quickly can you repeat it correctly? Most likely right away. And if you can sing a rhythm, you can play it.

Rhythmic Language

The next series of exercises gives syllables to common rhythmic patterns. This idea is centuries old, stemming from the classical Indian tradition of rhythmic solfège. Before tabla students are allowed to learn the drum, they spend years vocally learning the rhythmic language of the music they will eventually play. This approach ensures that once the instrument's mechanics are mastered, the music comes from inside the musician. As bass players, this is our goal, too.

Let's work with two common levels of the rhythmic hierarchy: the 16th-note and the eighth-note triplet. The syllables will help you to internalize the rhythms' feel, and they'll also give you a "tag" to help you remember what they look like. We often see a rhythm and figure it out, only to have to figure it out again the next time it shows up—so giving rhythms tags helps you remember them visually.

It's important to realize how many rhythms you already know just from listening to modern music. The 16th-note, for example, is very common in rock, funk, Latin, jazz, and pop, so the sounds of 16th-note rhythms are deeply embedded in your musical consciousness. However, it's common for people to play such rhythms unevenly. Instead of precisely aligning them with the rhythmic grid, they're sprayed wildly around the bar like water spewing from a runaway garden hose.

Sing the rhythms in Ex. 13 with a metronome clicking quarter-notes. Keep in mind it's unimportant how well you sing; since this is a purely rhythmic exercise, so you can just speak the syllables. The syllables in parentheses are rests that need to be inserted in order to capture the groove. Feel the 16th-note pulse continuing through the rests on beats *two* and *four*. Or, if you're having trouble with that, fill them in silently with "dig-a-chik-a."

The triplet is the underlying rhythmic element of styles such as jazz, blues, and hip-hop. It's also the essence of swing. (If you thought "swing" was just a function on your drum machine, guess again.) Since eighth- and 16th-notes are divisible by two, they can be imagined as little square boxes that rotate in time. A triplet, however, is round and wave-like. If you divide 100 by 3, you get 33—with a small amount of "change," more like 33.333…the decimal places can continue ad infinitum. That remainder is why triplets are also very flexible; they can be stretched and compacted. This accounts for how two jazz drummers can play the same rhythm and still sound different—each one interprets the triplet in his own way. For the sake of clarity, we'll go for an even, relaxed, flowing triplet that sits in the middle of the beat. Ex. 14 shows a series of rhythmic patterns based on triplets. Sing the rest syllables, but accent the ones that are to be played. This will give you a better feel for the triplet. Remember: It's just as important to groove when playing rests as it is when playing notes.

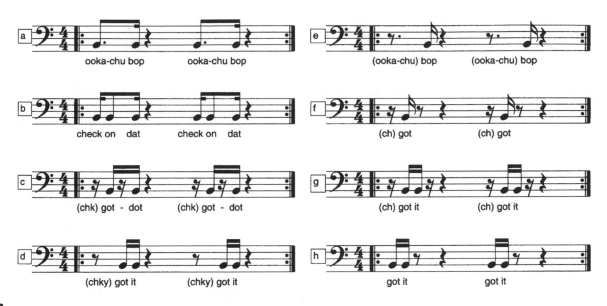

Ex. 13

On the Grid

Playing rhythm involves breaking the steady flow of time into specific units of measure. (This might sound like a math lesson, but don't be scared.) These units may vary in length according to the music's style or demands, but they all must line up to the time grid; this means all rhythms must exist within the prescribed tempo of music you're playing. (We're talking about groove-oriented bass playing, not free-form jazz.) Accordingly, I've developed a concept of the rhythmic hierarchy I call

Ex. 14

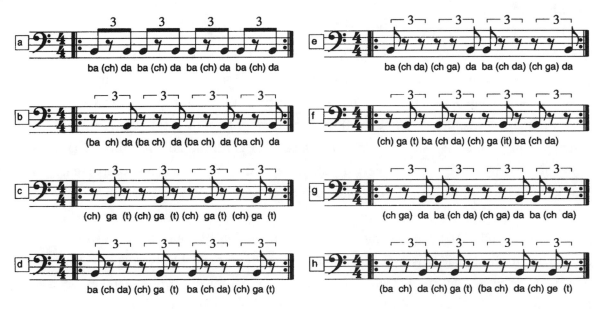

"the grid." For the sake of keeping this manageable, we'll discuss only note values from whole-notes to 16th-note triplets—but be aware that the information also applies to longer and shorter notes.

Ex. 15 shows the rhythmic hierarchy. Notice how all the levels of rhythmic activity are connected. A group of four 16th-notes takes up the same space on the time grid as two eighth-notes or the three notes of an eighth-note triplet. This means that the amount of space for any given rhythmic grouping is set and non-negotiable. Four 16th-notes get as much space as they get—no more, no less.

Playing these different rhythmic levels can be challenging, because the shorter the rhythmic values, the more opportunities you have to get off track. But there's an old saying: "The faster you play, the slower you count." In other words, if you're playing lots of short notes, you should count *longer* time values, both to prevent losing the pulse and to maintain a strong groove. So if you're playing 16th-notes, you could count eighth-notes—but that isn't slow enough to keep the feel grounded. The groove needs to come from a deeper place. So in that situation you should count half-notes, as shown in Ex. 16. To do that you'll need to function on several rhythmic levels at once—something drummers do all the time.

Play some of your cool, busy slap licks, but instead of tapping your foot on every quarter-note, tap it on every half-note. Tapping your foot more slowly relaxes you and removes the anxiety of having to play at a fast tempo. It also helps anchor the 16th-notes to the time grid, which makes them easier to play. This will take some getting used to, but once you settle into it, you'll find your 16th-notes feel more relaxed and your grooves fall into the pocket more easily.

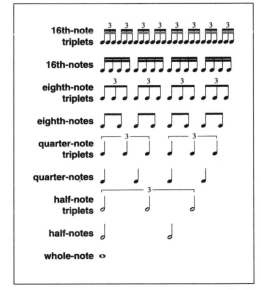

Ex. 15

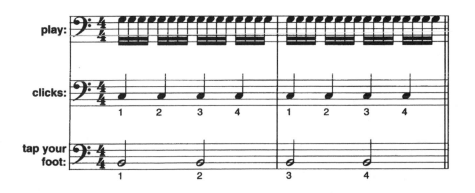

Ex. 16

Go with the Flow

Practicing all these exercises with the metronome as well as with and without your instrument will solidify your internal grid connection. Rhythm is generated by the seamless meshing of our internal clock with the gears of the ever-moving time continuum. Like the inside of a fine pocket watch, time and rhythm exist in a synchronous unity. Each level of rhythmic activity exists on its own plane, yet it's simultaneously linked to every other plane of rhythm as well. Take rhythm inside, and your bass playing will groove with the flow of the universe.

Chapter 2

Navigating a Chord Chart

Reading music is an important aspect of total musicianship, and if you want to become a professional player—particularly as a freelancer—it's an absolute must. Most people think of reading music as the ability to rip through densely covered pages of syncopated 16th-notes. Certainly that skill will serve you well at some point in your career. Most of the time, though, you'll be given either a chord chart (chord symbols with slashes indicating the number of beats per measure and perhaps some rhythmic kicks) or a lead sheet (the melody of a song with chord symbols written above each measure).

With this information you'll be expected to create something appropriate to the style you're playing. That should be pretty easy, you may think—it's certainly less strenuous than sight-reading Bach cello suites—but those little chord symbols contain a lot of information.

Chord Construction

A prerequisite to understanding chord symbols is knowing how different chord types are constructed. If you aren't familiar with this information, there's a column called "construction" in the chord-symbol listings that follow; it tells you how the chords are built. Practice playing the chords as arpeggios, from the root to the top note and back down. Also, play each chord starting on different roots until you've played every chord type in every key.

To get started, you need to know what a chord symbol tells you directly. The root is the most obvious piece of information. The symbol also tells you whether the chord is major or minor; what type of 7th (if any) it has; whether the 5th is perfect, flatted, or raised; and whether there are any additional tones to be considered, such as a suspended 4th or upper extensions (9, 11, 13).

As shown in Fig. 1, a chord symbol is divided into two parts: the prefix and the suffix. (For those of you who slept through English class, the prefix is the first part, the suffix the last.) The prefix is all that is used for triads; the suffix gets used in four-part (and larger) chords.

Fig. 1

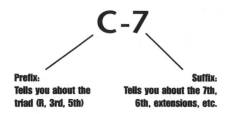

Fig. 2 shows the five basic prefixes used for all chord symbols; the "also seen as" column lists other ways (both correct and incorrect) you'll see the chord written.

Fig. 2

Symbol	Name	Construction	Also Seen As
C	C major triad	R–3–5–(8)	CM
	Note: A chord is always major unless you see a minor (m or –), diminished (dim or °), augmented (aug or +) or sus symbol		
C–	C minor triad	R–♭3–5–(8)	Cm, Cmin
C°	C diminished triad	R–♭3–♭5–(8)	Cdim
C+	C augmented triad	R–3–♯5–(8)	Caug
Csus	C suspended 4	R–4–5–(8)	Csus4

Now let's look at the suffixes. It's important to be able to visually separate the suffix from the prefix; when you see the symbol C–7, for example, the minor symbol (–) pertains to the triad (C–E♭–G), not the 7th (B♭). When you see a plain numeral 7 in a chord symbol, that indicates the 7th is a ♭7. (The ♭7 is sometimes called a minor 7th, but don't confuse that with a minor 7 chord). When you see *Cmaj7*, the *C* is the prefix, meaning it is a *C* major triad; the major symbol (maj) is part of the suffix and refers to the 7th. It indicates that the 7th is a major 7th, like the 7th note in a major scale (conveniently found a half-step below the octave root). This may be a little confusing at first, but you will be amazed how simple it is to read chord symbols once you've spent some time practicing.

Fig. 3 is a table listing *C* chords with various common suffixes.

Fig. 3

Symbol	Name	Construction	Also Seen As
Cmaj7	C major 7	R–3–5–7	CM7, C$\triangle$7
	C major triad, with the 7th scale degree from the major scale		
C7	C7, or "dominant 7"	R–3–5–$\flat$7	
	C major triad, with a minor or flatted 7th		
C–7	C minor 7	R–$\flat$3–5–$\flat$7	Cm7, Cmin7
	C minor triad, with a minor or flatted 7th		
C–7($\flat$5)	C minor 7 flat 5	R–$\flat$3–$\flat$5–$\flat$7	Cm7$\flat$5, C–7$\flat$5, C$\emptyset$, C$\emptyset$7
	C diminished triad, with a minor or flatted 7th		
	(sometimes called a "half diminished" chord)		
C–(maj7)	C minor major 7	R–$\flat$3–5–7	Cmmaj7, C–$\triangle$7
	C minor triad, with the 7th scale degree from the major scale		
C°7	C diminished 7	R–$\flat$3–$\flat$5–$\flat\flat$7	Cdim7
	C diminished triad, with a diminished, or "double flatted" 7th		
	(the double flatted 7th is actually the 6th scale degree)		
C+7	C augmented 7	R–3–$\sharp$5–$\flat$7	Caug7, C7$\sharp$5, C7+5
	C augmented triad, with a minor, or flatted 7th		
C+maj7	C augmented major 7	R–3–$\sharp$5–7	Caugmaj7, Cmaj7$\sharp$5, Cmaj7+5
	C augmented triad, with the 7th scale degree from the major scale		
Csus7	C7 suspended 4	R–4–5–$\flat$7	C7sus
	C suspended triad, with a minor or flatted 7th		
C6	C6	R–3–5–6	C13
	C major triad, with the 6th scale degree from the major scale		
C6/9	C6/9	R–3–6–9	C(9/13)
	C major triad, usually with the 6th scale degree substituting for the 5th, with extension 9 on top		
C–6	C minor 6	R–$\flat$3–5–6	Cm6, Cmin6
	C minor triad, with the 6th scale degree from the major scale		

Ex. 1 shows the different arpeggios written out for you to practice. In addition to knowing them from the root up, you'll need to know where on the fingerboard you can find all the notes each chord contains. First I'll write the arpeggio in order from the bottom note to the top. Next I'll write out each arpeggio from the lowest bass note possible to the highest, using a 24-fret 4-string bass as a reference. Remember that many of the notes can be found in different places on the fingerboard, so exper-

Ex. 1

iment with placement. Don't forget to practice these in all keys! This is a lot of work, but a pro bassist needs to know this information.

You will also encounter chord symbols that indicate bass notes that are different from the roots. In these symbols the chord and the bass note are separated by a slash. These alternate bass notes may be chord tones or non-chord tones. For example, *C7/G*, which indicates a *C7* chord with a *G* in the bass, can be considered a *C7* inversion with the 5th (*G*) on the bottom. However, the *F♯* in the chord *C7/F♯* is a truly alternate bass note. The *F♯* is not part of the original chord but is used to create a particular harmonic effect. In either case, you should approach this type of chord by playing the specified bass note. (If you're improvising a solo, base your ideas on top chord, and use the alternate bass note as an additional tone.)

Now that you understand basic chord anatomy, look at the chord chart in Ex. 2.

It's typical of one you might encounter on a gig. In addition to the chords, this chart contains rhythmic notation as well as some common "road map" features, such as first and second endings, repeat signs, and rehearsal letters.

In the upper-left-hand corner is the style marking. In this case it says "Swing," which means you should play a walking line. The chart gives you only basic information about the song; the exact feel is up to the rhythm section. Listen to the kick-drum rhythm to get a sense of the basic feel, and catch the rhythms I've indicated on the chart. (As an exercise, once you've gone through the chart as a swing tune, play it as if the style marking said "Afro pop," "half-time funk," or "12/8 shuffle." These are just a few of this progression's possible interpretations.)

The large letters **A** and **B** inside rectangles are called rehearsal marks or rehearsal letters; they indicate the tune's form. In this case, the song has an **A** section and a **B** section (bridge), and overall one of the most common forms, **AABA**.

The repeat signs tell you more about the form. In this case, start at the top (bar 1) and play through the first ending; then repeat back to the top, as indicated by the double bar plus two vertical dots. Play until you reach the point where the first-ending sign starts, skip those two bars, and go directly to the second ending. Then play through the second ending and go on to the bridge (B section). The last A section goes straight through to the double bar line; this is the end of the form. (Each time through the form is called a "chorus.") To continue the song, go back to the top.

The last bar contains *D–7* and *G7* in parentheses; this means they're the turn-around, which takes you back to the top. When you end the song, they are to be left out and replaced with an ending. As is the case with most charts, there is no specific ending indicated; it's up to the band to come up with an ending that begins in the second-to-last bar. There are several choices, but I chose Ex. 3, the No. 1 favorite,

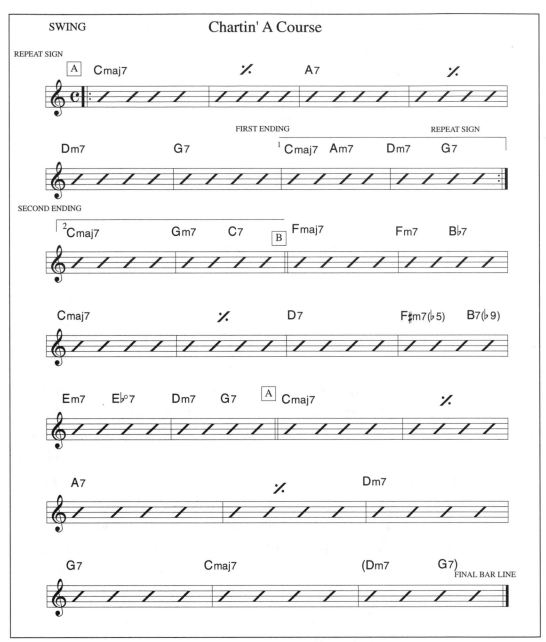

super-duper, can't miss, greatest ending of all time. The tune will play through two choruses on the CD. The first time through take the turnaround to the top. The second time through, replace the last two measures with the ending. The dotted semicircle over the last note is called a fermata. This symbol tells you to hold the last note until the bandleader signals a cutoff. This is usually done with a nod of the head ("head cue").

Ex. 3

Extensions

Some chord symbols contain information about upper extensions ("tensions"), such as ♭9, ♯9, ♯11, and ♭13. These symbols indicate tones built on top of the triad or 7th chord. Tension 9 is actually scale degree 2, up an octave. Tension 11 is scale degree 4 up an octave, and tension 13 is scale degree 6. Typically, these extensions will alter your choice of passing tones as you move though a chord. For example, a ♭9 in a chord symbol indicates you use a ♭2 passing tone instead of natural 2. Ex. 4 shows a C7♭9♭13 chord with its appropriate scale. The chord tones are in bold.

Ex. 4

There are also symbols that indicate a specific scale to use; for instance, C7alt tells you to use an altered scale (Ex. 5). The altered scale is unusual. It has ♭9 and ♯9 tensions, and the chord's major 3rd is the altered scale's fourth tone. The scale also contains the ♭5 chord tone and ♭13 tension.

Ex. 5

In addition, each chord symbol implies one or more scales appropriate for a given chord. Depending on the progression and the key, one or all of those scale possibilities may change. For example, in the key of C major, a D–7 is the II–7 chord and would take the D Dorian scale. In the key of B♭ major, a D–7 is the III–7 and would take the D Phrygian scale (Ex. 6).

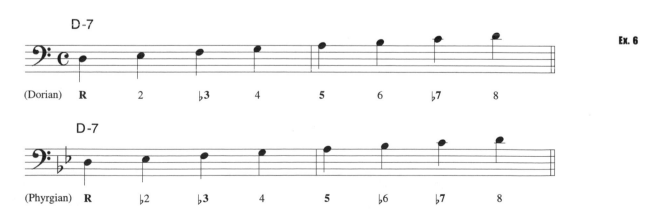

Ex. 6

You may encounter a poorly written fake book with horribly wrong chord changes (that may also be illegible), and you'll have to figure out the right thing to play. Sometimes fake books have improper root motion; if so, the piano player might decide to play what he thinks is right and not tell anyone else. (For you, this is called on-the-job training.)

As you gain experience in these situations, you'll be able to figure out what's happening. In the meantime, practice all of your arpeggios in all keys until they're second nature. Study the tables in this chapter and become familiar with all the symbols and the various ways they can be written. Practice reading the changes from a fake book or sheet music. Although you may need to play only the root much of the time, knowing about the rest of the chord will help you create lines and fills that make sense. When you get tired of playing by yourself, find some other musicians, open up a book, and read through those changes!

Chapter **3**

Training Your Ears

Some musicians have "good ears," some don't. Players with good ears can get through almost any musical challenge on the spot. They can learn tunes on the bandstand, instantly tell a song's key, find the right notes to play, and easily transpose songs to new keys. Players with bad ears, however, make a gig more difficult for everyone. They have trouble figuring out simple chord progressions, can't find notes that work with the song, and seem to get in the way a lot. Needless to say, these players are not the first to get called. To be the best musician you can be, you must be able to know what you want to play and how it works with the rest of the music. Why waste time fishing around for the right notes when you can learn to hear and find them instantly?

While some people seem born with "magic ears," you can develop that skill like anything else. Through ear training, you can learn to identify pitches, intervals, chord structures, and rhythms. Once you start doing this, you'll realize you are on a lifelong journey—one that started long ago, well before you ever became a musician. You can hum "Twinkle, Twinkle, Little Star," right? That's because you began training your ears when you were little. A big part of becoming a skilled musician is to continue this training on a much more sophisticated level. The examples in this chapter will be challenging at first but in time will become easy. That's when you must search out more difficult material. Once you've identified an example, the challenge is gone. Use these exercises as an introduction, then find new sources. Ear training is an endless subject—you can always improve.

Diatonic Intervals

Before you can expect to hear complex harmonies, you need to start with simple intervals. An interval is the space between two notes. We identify intervals using the major scale as a reference; each note in the scale is numbered one through eight. The first note played (or the bottom note if the notes are played simultaneously) becomes the root; from there, count up or down the major scale to find the interval's size. If you count up three notes in the scale, it's called a 3rd; four notes is a 4th, and so on. Of course, not all intervals are within the major scale; some occur between scale tones. We'll first look at the intervals within the major scale; these are called *diatonic*.

The diatonic intervals are divided into major and perfect intervals; these can be lowered or raised, resulting in minor, augmented and diminished intervals. In Fig. 1 I've listed the intervals and their alterations with the theoretically correct names. Beneath some I've included alternate (enharmonic) names for them. For example, raising a major 3rd by a half-step technically gives you an "augmented 3rd," but it's commonly called a perfect 4th, as Fig. 1 shows.

Fig. 1

	Interval	Distance in half-steps	Lowered by a half-step becomes...	Raised by a half-step becomes...
Perfect	unison	0	N.A.	minor second
	fourth	5	diminished fourth	augmented fourth
	fifth	7	diminished fifth	augmented fifth
	octave	12	major seventh	minor ninth
Major	second	2	minor second	augmented second
	third	4	minor third	perfect fourth
	sixth	9	minor sixth	augmented sixth
	seventh	11	minor seventh	octave

For the sake of simplicity, musicians often refer to intervals with alternate names such "♭2" for the minor 2nd or "♯5" for the augmented 5th. This gets the meaning across and saves valuable brain activity, which is better reserved for creating music.

In addition to representing intervals with numbers, we also use traditional solfège syllables: do, re, mi, fa, sol, la, ti, do. These designate the different scale degrees: "do" refers to the first degree, "re" refers to the second, etc. Ex. 1 shows the *F* major scale ascending and descending; beneath the notes there's a row of numbers, then the syllables, and then another row of numbers. Each number in the top row indicates the interval number ascending from the low *F* and then descending from the upper *F*. We use the ascending intervals as our template for naming intervals. The distance between scale tones 1 and 3 is called a major 3rd, and the precise distance is four half-steps. However, when you go back down the major scale, the resulting descending 3rd (between the octave and scale degree 6) is a *minor* 3rd (♭3)—the distance is three half-steps. So to know the interval you have to count the number of half-steps it comprises. The bottom row shows the scale-degree number. Notice how these numbers run in opposite order of the descending intervals. For example, the C below the upper *F* is the 5th scale degree, but the interval between the two notes is a (descending) 4th.

Ex. 1

Intervals:	1	2	3	4	5	6	7	8	1	♭2	♭3	4	5	♭6	♭7	8
Syllables:	Do	Re	Mi	Fa	Sol	La	Ti	Do	Do	Ti	La	Sol	Fa	Mi	Re	Do
Scale:	1	2	3	4	5	6	7	8	8	7	6	5	4	3	2	1

Ex. 2 will help you learn to hear every interval both ascending and descending. The intervals are written out twice, in ascending and then descending order. Play the first pair of notes in each measure while singing along, but then sing the second pair unaccompanied. If you have access to a piano, play these intervals for yourself until you really have them down; but also play them on your bass. It's important to relate the sounds to your instrument. Play the low *F* on the *E* string, and then play the next note up. Listen carefully to the sound of the interval, and sing it using the appropriate solfège syllable. Continue until you have played and sung each ascending interval, and then repeat the process descending. Do this in all keys.

The bass's range is lower than most people can sing, so sing up an octave if you need to. If your bass has a two-octave neck or if you're using a piano, play everything up an octave. Still, many people hit a stumbling block when asked to sing. If you're insecure about singing aloud, I have some advice: First, take five deep, long breaths to relax, and then *get over it!* Do you want to get your ears together or not? If you do, learn to *sing* what you hear! You don't have to sound like Pavarotti—for now, just get close enough to the pitch so it's discernible. If you must, wait until no one else is home. After you have sung intervals for a while, it becomes comfortable. You may even start to like it.

TRACK
3

Ex. 2

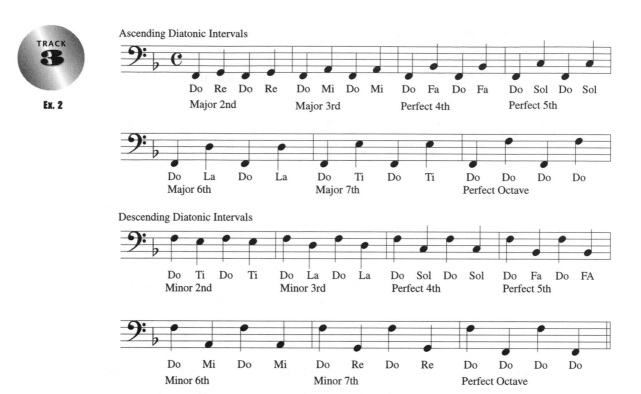

It's important to make a list of mnemonic "tags" to help you recall the ascending and descending intervals. Once you have listened to and sung each interval, find a familiar tune that uses that interval, and write it down. For example, you can recall a major 2nd interval by singing the first two notes of "Do, a Deer" from *The Sound of Music*. Similarly, you can recall a major 3rd by singing "Michael Row Your Boat Ashore," and a perfect 5th by singing "Twinkle, Twinkle, Little Star." These references may not be very hip, but they are memorable, and that's what counts. Time spent considering each interval's sound will pay off when you have to hear your way through an unfamiliar tune on the gig. Find musical references for all the diatonic intervals; look for easy, can't-miss tunes, and you'll be in good shape.

Once you have sung through the ascending and descending intervals, move on to Ex. 3. Start on the root and sing the entire scale "do" to "do," ascending and descending. Then start on the second scale note and sing "re" to "re." Repeat from each note in the scale. (You will be singing the diatonic major modes.)

Next, sing the diatonic arpeggios from the major scale. Ex. 4 shows the major-scale arpeggios written out with their solfège syllables. Sing all of these exercises in every key. Not only do you need to hear the intervals and the chord structures, you need to hear each key's unique sound.

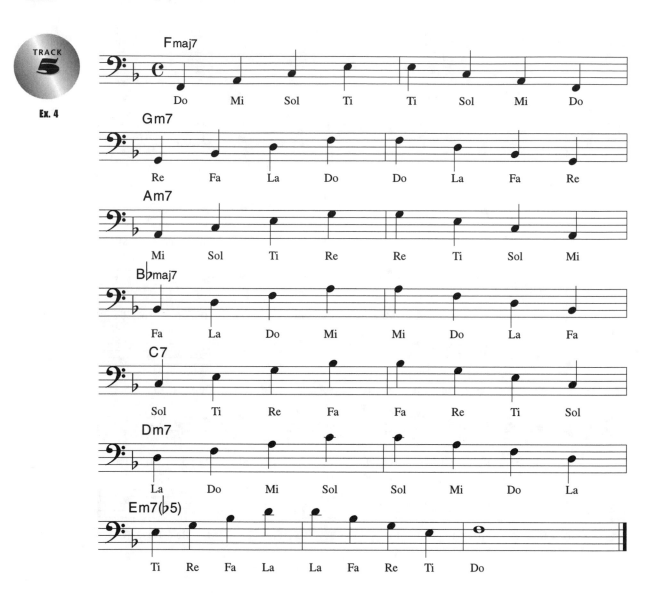

Once you've practiced singing the intervals, modes, and arpeggios with an instrument to guide you, do it without one. Get your starting pitch from the bass or piano, and then sing each exercise unaccompanied using the solfège syllables. Practice this *a lot*—it's essential to your musical development.

Chromatic Intervals

Between the scale tones are *chromatic* pitches. Using the F major scale as a reference, this time we'll include the chromatic pitches (Ex. 5). I've given you the solfège syllables and scale-degree numbers; as before, pay attention to the directions the numbers run. Ascending, the chromatic solfège syllables change to a long "e" sound, spelled with an "i" (Fig. 2). Descending, the vowels change again; some syllables use an "e" pronounced with a long "a" sound (as in "cake"), others an "a" pronounced as in "mama" (Fig. 3). Fig. 4 shows the complete list of chromatic syllables, ascending and descending. As with the diatonic major intervals, practice playing and singing these in both directions.

The Chromatic Scale

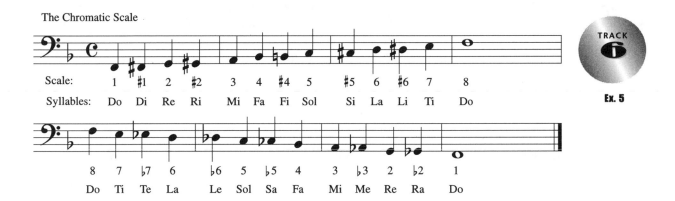

| Scale: | 1 | #1 | 2 | #2 | 3 | 4 | #4 | 5 | #5 | 6 | #6 | 7 | 8 |
| Syllables: | Do | Di | Re | Ri | Mi | Fa | Fi | Sol | Si | La | Li | Ti | Do |

| 8 | 7 | ♭7 | 6 | ♭6 | 5 | ♭5 | 4 | 3 | ♭3 | 2 | ♭2 | 1 |
| Do | Ti | Te | La | Le | Sol | Sa | Fa | Mi | Me | Re | Ra | Do |

TRACK
6

Ex. 5

Fig. 2
Ascending Chromatic Solfège Syllables

Major Scale Tone	Chromatic Scale Tone (one half-step up)
do	di ("dee")
re ("ray")	ri
mi ("mee")	N.A.
fa	fi
sol	si
la	li
ti	N.A.

Fig. 3
Descending Chromatic Solfège Syllables

Major Scale Tone	Chromatic Scale Tone (one half-step down)
do	N.A.
ti	te ("tay")
la	le
sol	sa
fa	N.A.
mi	me
re	ra

Fig. 4
Chromatic Solfège Syllables—Complete Set

ascending = do, di, re, ri, mi, fa, fi, sol, si, la, li, ti, do
descending = do, ti, te, la, le, sol, sa, fa, mi, me, re, ra, do

Once you have a handle on the chromatic intervals and their corresponding syllables, learn to hear the minor scales. The three basic minor scales are natural minor (also known as the Aeolian mode), melodic minor, and harmonic minor. Ex. 6 shows the solfège syllables for the natural minor scale. Even though you already sang through the natural minor scale earlier as the "la" to "la" Aeolian mode, it's important to learn it as a scale unto itself—so you should learn the syllables from "do" to "do" as well. The chromatic solfège alterations tell you very specifically how the scale is built. The syllable "me" means a ♭3, "le" means a ♭6, and "te" a ♭7. Go back to all of the modes built from the major scale and sing them individually with each scale's first note being "do," making the necessary chromatic alterations to the syllables.

Intervals:	1	2	♭3	4	5	♭6	♭7	8	1	2	3	4	5	6	♭7	8
Syllables:	Do	Re	Me	Fa	Sol	Le	Te	Do	Do	Te	Le	Sol	Fa	Me	Re	Do
Scale:	1	2	♭3	4	5	♭6	♭7	8	8	♭7	♭6	5	4	♭3	2	1

Ex. 6

You've already sung the diatonic arpeggios of natural minor. They're the same ones built from the major scale, but in a different order. The other minor scales are not derivative of any other scale, so they have their own sets of diatonic modes and arpeggios.

Ex. 7 shows the melodic minor scale with its solfège syllables. Except for the all-important ♭3 ("me"), this scale has the same notes as the major scale.

Intervals:	♭2	2	♭3	4	5	6	7	8	1	♭2	♭3	4	5	6	♭7	8
Syllables:	Do	Re	Me	Fa	Sol	La	Ti	Do	Do	Ti	La	Sol	Fa	Me	Re	Do
Scale:	1	2	♭3	4	5	6	7	8	8	7	6	5	4	♭3	2	1

Ex. 7

Ex. 8 shows the diatonic modes from the melodic minor scale. Notice the names are alterations on the diatonic major modes. This helps us develop a sense of how they are built. Sing them with the syllables written, and then learn them using "do" for the first syllable of each scale.

TRACK 9

EX. 8

Ex. 9 shows the diatonic arpeggios from melodic minor. Remember that each of the previous modes will correspond to the arpeggio built from the same scale degree. Also remember you need to sing these scales and arpeggios in all keys. I have not written out accompaniment in *all* keys, but you can do this on piano or simply a pitch pipe to give you a starting note. Having accompaniment is helpful, but ultimately you must learn to hear the sounds in your head, without help.

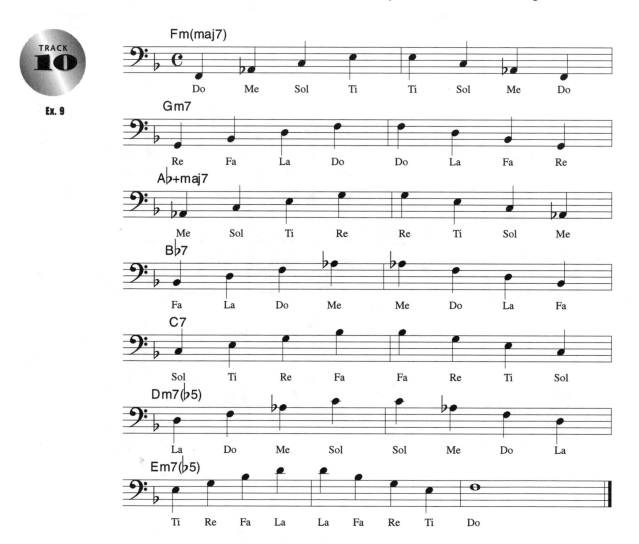

Ex. 10 shows the harmonic minor scale. The ♭6 ("le") and ♮7 ("ti") create the scale's characteristic minor 3rd leap. This unusual skip creates a Middle Eastern quality that makes for some interesting modes and arpeggios.

Example 11 shows the diatonic modes built off harmonic minor. Again, sing each mode with the supplied syllables *and* starting each scale on "do."

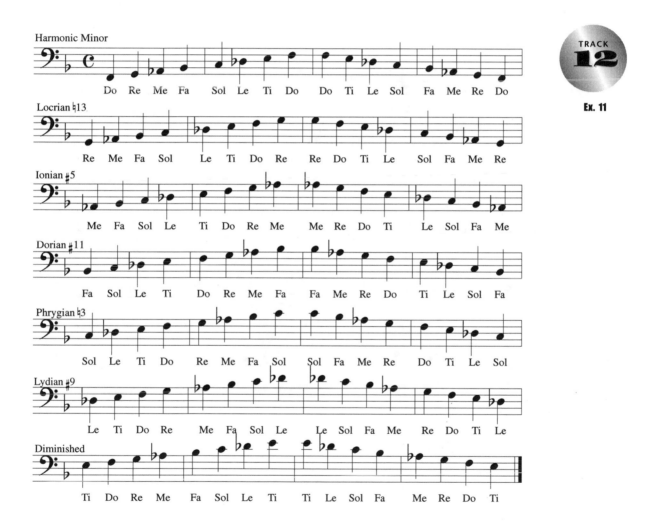

Example 12 shows the diatonic arpeggios built from harmonic minor.

While this may seem exhaustive, it only scratches the surface of what you need to do for ear training.

Identifying Pitches and Intervals

The next step involves learning to identify sounds. If you do all of the following activities, you will see amazing results in your ability to hear and understand music. The examples on the CD will give you some opportunities to test your ears, and you will find the answer key at the end of this chapter. For additional practice get a keyboardist or guitarist to help. If you can't, you can make your own practice tapes—but be sure to put enough material on each so you can't "cheat" and remember what you had recorded. Another option is to buy prerecorded ear-training tapes or get programs for your computer. (See page 38–39.)

We'll start with hearing single notes (Track 14). First I'll play a *C* to give your ear a reference point, then I'll play the new pitch. Each new note will be played two times; if you need to hear the note more than that, just rewind. By the third listening you should be confirming that you have the right pitch. There will be 11 different pitches played. On your bass, find each note you hear; if the note is played too high or too low for your range, find it in another octave. Write down your answers and check them with the bass or a piano.

Next we'll play two notes in a row, staying within one octave (Track 15). Find both pitches on the bass, and say aloud what interval they form. You'll get a *C* for reference, and then 12 examples repeated twice. Write down the names of the pitches and the interval they form, and check them.

Now we'll move on to three-note sequences (Track 16). After the reference *C* you'll hear 10 examples repeated twice. Write down the pitches, and check your answers.

The next group gives four-note sequences (Track 17). You'll hear the reference *C* and then ten examples, repeated twice.

The longer the string of notes you can hear and recall, the better. To create another exercise, go back to CD Track 14 and pick an interval—for example, a 5th. When you hear a note played, play a 5th above or below the note. Use all the different intervals. This may seem extremely difficult at first, but the more you do it, the easier it gets. It's easy to see how developing this skill will help you on the gig. This exercise is called melodic dictation, and it's a starting point for learning how to transcribe music. Eventually you can work your way up to four-bar and eight-bar phrases. The key is to focus on singing back the musical phrase to yourself as soon as possible after hearing it. If you can sing it, you will remember it. After that, writing it down becomes a process of simply determining your starting pitch and figuring out everything else in relation to that first note.

Next I'll play two notes simultaneously (Track 18). The interval will be within one octave. After your reference *C* you'll hear eight examples, repeated twice. On your bass, find the two notes and play the interval they create. Mentally refer back to your "tags" to you help identify the intervals. Write down the intervals as you hear them, and check your answers.

Identifying Chords

Once you're comfortable hearing intervals, it's time to start working on triads (Track 19). Now I'll play major, minor, diminished, and augmented triads in root position (with the root as the bottom note). I'll give eight examples, preceded by a *C* reference. First play them back on the bass, and then write them down. Make sure you write down the proper root for each chord type. Pay attention to each triad's unique sound.

After you have the triads down we'll work on four-part 7th chords in root position. I'll play major 7, minor 7, minor 7♭5, dominant 7, diminished 7, augmented 7, and augmented major 7 chords (Track 20). As always, you'll hear the reference *C*, and then 14 examples in root position. (I've added an additional root one octave lower than the rest of the chord to help you hear the bottom note). Listen for the 3rd. That note determines whether a chord is major or minor. You can almost take the 5th for granted, unless it's a ♭5 or ♯5, in which case the chord will sound distinctive. The 7th is the top note; along with the 3rd, it determines the chord type. Pay attention to each note in a voicing, and hear how the notes interact.

Inversions

Once you have a handle on root-position triads and 7th chords, you must be able to hear them in various inversions (Track 21). First inversion puts the 3rd on the bottom; instead of the structure being root–3–5 (from bottom to top), it becomes 3–5–root, with the root an octave higher. Inversions are very important. Pianists and guitarists often play chords this way, so you need to know the difference between an *Em* triad and a *C* triad in first inversion. I'll play the different triads (in *C*) in first inversion. Sing them, find them on your bass, and then write them down.

The second-inversion structure from bottom to top is 5–root–3 (Track 22). I'll repeat the process with various second-inversion triads (again in *C*).

Now I'll mix them up—some triads in first inversion, some in second (Track 23).

When you have a grasp on the triads, tackle the 7th chords. Because there are four notes in a 7th chord, there are now three inversions along with root position:

First inversion = 3–5–7–root

Second inversion = 5–7–root–3

Third inversion = 7–root–3–5

Now I'll play all of the 7th chords (in *C*) you've learned in each inversion (Track 24). I'll pick one chord type and play it in each inversion, from first to third. Sing through these inversions (use the correct syllables), play them on the bass, and write them down!

After a while you'll be able to tell each chord's characteristic sound in all inversions. Write down your answers and check them.

Progressions

Now let's work on chord progressions. I'll start by playing simple two-chord progressions (Track 25). The root motion will always be on the bottom, but some of the piano voicings above the root will be inversions. Listen first for the root motion and determine the interval between the roots. Then listen for the 3rds. Are the chords major or minor? Listen for the top notes to determine what type of 7th the chords have. If you hear something unique in the middle of the voicing, listen for a ♭5 or ♯5. There will be five examples. Replay them as many times as you need, and check your work in the answer key.

Now we'll try some four-chord progressions (Track 26). I'll give five examples, each repeated twice. Use the same steps to determine root motion and chord type.

With the help of a friend or a computer program, work up to four-bar and eight-bar progressions, and then move on to progressions with the chords in inversions. As you get the hang of this, you'll be able to play along with new chord progressions in tempo. This is what bassists are often required to do in the real world—play along to new songs on the spot, without written music.

Continuous Ear Training

Developing your ears can be a part of daily life. You're constantly surrounded by opportunities to use them analytically. Carry a pitch pipe and practice tuning your ears to a particular note. The most common reference tone is *A*, but learn to recall all

Ear Training Answer Key

Ear Training Answers p. 2

the other notes, too. Emphasize your open-string notes: *E, A, D,* and *G.* During the day, periodically test your pitch recall against the pitch pipe. You can also use a tuning fork; since it gives you only one note, it becomes more of a challenge to find the others. Pick a note from the pitch pipe and sing major and minor scales, intervals, and arpeggios in that key. Use the solfège syllables!

Whenever you listen to music, exercise your ears. Simply enjoying it isn't enough—you must learn to understand what you hear. Write down information about a favorite song. What key is it in? What is the first melody note? What is that note in relationship to the first chord (a root, 3rd, 5th, etc.)? What is the interval between the first two melody notes? Does the song change keys? What is the chord progression? The time signature? What instruments are playing the melody and the solos? What instruments are in the rhythm section? Also, play bass along with the radio—whatever comes on! Switch around to different stations with different types of music. Listen for random sounds throughout the day—car horns, yells, passing radios—and identify the pitches you hear.

While all of this may seem fanatical, the pursuit of musical excellence is a full-time occupation; you will need to become obsessed with learning to hear musically. Once you have reached a certain level, you'll find it much easier and more enjoyable to practice these skills. The bottom line: Your musical worth is directly proportional to your ability to hear well. Good ears make you a valuable player. If you have chosen to be a serious musician, it is your absolute duty to train your ears—so what are you doing sitting around reading a book? Get to work!

▪ Noted Bassists Sound Off on Ear Training ▪

Larry Ridley: Some people are locked into processing information from what they see, and they don't develop their ears. On a gig you have to just go ahead and play, so you must have big enough ears to deal with that. When someone calls a tune it doesn't matter whether you know it—you just have to *play.*

Rufus Reid: You have to learn how to use your ears and relate what you hear to what the bass is supposed to do. I know students who can play *all* over the bass; they're incredible technicians, but they can't play something they hear someone else play. My first real shocker was playing with Buddy Montgomery. He didn't read music, so if I wanted to keep the gig I had to learn to hear fast and to remember and recall. It's a survival technique.

Michael Moore: One of the biggest problems of being a bass player is we're expected to know every song ever written, but they never ask us to call one! I tell students to put on a Frank Sinatra record—he recorded every great standard—and play along. Or take 15 minutes a day, turn on the radio, and find the bass parts. That's what we're doing most of the time—relying on our ears.

The more I play the piano the better my ear gets. When I hear a pianist play a chord, I know what it is just by the sound of the instrument—I've played that voicing myself. The keyboard makes it much more concrete.

■ Ear-Training Computer Programs ■

Not many of us know a pianist or guitarist willing to endlessly pound out intervals, arpeggios, and chord progressions for our ear-training sessions. But if you have a computer, you're in luck—there are many commercial and shareware programs that can save you from having to mow your pianist's lawn for the next decade. Here are a few programs I've checked out for Macintosh as well as some online sources for PC-based programs. There are also some Web sites that can help you find other programs and book/CD packages.

Ear Training on the Web

A good place to start is **www.shareware.com**. Type in "ear training," and you'll find a slew of links to various Web sites. Some highlights:

www.upbeat.com/caris/eartrain.htm
Caris Music Services offers several text/CD packages, including *Training the Ear* by Armen Donelian. This 158-page book comes with two CDs or cassettes for $40. *Ear Training Vol. 1* by Sigi Busch, a 47-page workbook with CD, sells for $25. *Ear Training* by Tom Van Der Geld, a 190-page book with three CDs, sells for $40.

cctr.umkc.edu/user/bauera/et.html
"First Aid for Ear Straining and Vexation." Links to various ear-training and theory-related sites.

www.miditec.com/home.html
Ear Master 2.0 is an advanced ear-training program for Windows 95 and Windows 3.1. It contains exercises for chords, intervals, scales, rhythm, and melodies, with definable skill levels. Thirty-day free trial.

kapitan.biostat.wiscedu/musicp2.html
This is a standalone program designed to parallel the fifth edition of *Ear Training: A Technique for Listening* by

Bruce Benward and Timothy Kolosick [Brown & Benchmark]. It requires Windows 3.1 or higher, a VGA or EGA monitor, Windows MIDI-out driver, and MIDI tone generator.

If you're a Macintosh user on AOL, you can find several shareware programs by following this path: computers & software/Mac software center/music & sound/applications & utilities/music applications & utilities/Mac music applications. Here are a few I checked out:

Ear Training 2.4 by Lars Peters
This great program allows you to choose from a list of scales, intervals, chords, and pitch identifications to drill on. You can choose intervals that occur within an octave, within two octaves, ascending, descending, or played simultaneously. It plays ascending and descending arpeggios as well as chords. The scale list includes all the major modes, some of the minor modes, pentatonic, symmetrical diminished, and three user-defined scales. You can adjust the speed of the examples played. It supports MIDI and QuickTime. For a $20 registration fee, you can keep your shareware karma clean.

Chord Lab 1.3.2 by Arthur Roolf
This shareware program focuses on chord structures and allows you to customize your ear-training sessions. It uses MIDI or QuickTime sounds for playback. You can check out some of its features free, and for $15 you can register and use the entire program.

Goats Intervals 2.1 by Marion Williamson
Shareware program focusing on interval drills. The author requests a $10 user fee on the honor system. You can choose which intervals you want to work on. One small drawback is intervals of more than an octave are not represented as compound intervals on the drill interface; if the program plays a major 10th, you have to answer "major 3rd" to be correct.

Melodic Ear Trainer 1.3 by David Bagno
A simple melodic-practice program that allows you to choose a series of pitches from one to six notes; it plays the pitches and shows them on the staff. You then click an onscreen piano keyboard for the correct answer. The program has speech capability. (The default settings use the "whisper" voice from the standard voice set—it's like having Freddy Krueger as an ear-training instructor!) The program eerily encourages you when you're correct, and when you mess up it tells you to concentrate harder. Trying to change the voice to something more pleasant caused my computer to freeze up—I suggest turning off the voice completely. For a real challenge, turn off the "show notes" function and identify the pitches by ear alone.

Ear Master Pro 4.0
This Windows-only program costs $69 and offers a three-week free trial. The **Ear Master School** version is designed for teachers. **www.earmaster.com**

One store-bought program I have used with success is Ars Nova's **Practica Musica**, a comprehensive workout for the ears and brain. It supports MIDI and internal sounds. The activities include pitch matching, pitch reading, rhythm matching, rhythm reading, pitch and rhythm reading, scales and key signatures, interval playing, interval spelling, interval ear training, chord playing, chord spelling, chord ear training, chord progression ear training, pitch dictation, rhythmic dictation, pitch and rhythmic dictation, and melody writing and listening. Whew! You can customize all activities to match your ability level. The program uses either a guitar fretboard, onscreen piano keyboard, or piano keyboard with a staff. The drills are set up as tests with a score needed for completion. This program is a serious tool that can challenge even the most advanced musician. Now available in version 4, it retails for $125 and can be ordered from Ars Nova Software, Box 637, Kirkland, WA 98083; (425) 889-0927; fax (425) 889-8699; **www.ars-nova.com**.

Comprehensive Ear Training is based on the requirements of Canada's Royal Conservatory of Music. The book is $9.95; book plus two cassettes, $24.95; book plus two CDs, $29.95; book plus MIDI disc, $29.95. Keystroke Publishing, Box 249, Sicamous, B.C., Canada V0E 2V0; (250) 836-3992; **www.keystrokepublishing.com**.

Gary Willis has some cool free ear training exercises up at www.garywillis.com. He has also written an excellent book/CD package, *Ultimate Ear Training for Guitar and Bass* [Hal Leonard]. It's broken down into three sections: 1. Manufacturing—internalizing the sound without an instrument. 2. Visualization—imagining the sound and shape on the fingerboard. 3. Imitation—internalizing, visualizing and playing the sound on your instrument. The course covers intervals, triads, chords, inversions, rhythms, melodic shapes, extensions, and alterations and can be ordered direct from the Web site for $15.

None of these programs was designed specifically for bassists, so you'll have to deal with a piano keyboard. But this is a good thing—it's very helpful to learn to relate to music in ways other than the fretboard, and the piano lays out the tones in a very systematic and visual way. Some programs have guitar fretboards available as an interface, which isn't a bad idea, either.

With any program, remember to start slowly; if you've never done ear-training work before, don't begin at the intermediate level. Small successes will build your confidence. If you feel overwhelmed, that's understandable. Just remember you *can* achieve good ears—all you need to do is practice and listen.

Section Two

Gig Survival

Chapter 4

Faking It

In addition to the right wardrobe, a working bassist needs several skills: good time, workable technique, knowledge of various styles, reading ability, good sound, good ears, and—very important—an extensive repertoire. But sooner or later you'll be called upon to "fake" a tune you don't know. Bandleaders want the freedom to call any tune they feel is appropriate, so if there's an odd request from someone flashing a $100 bill—or a weapon—you might have to fake it. It doesn't matter if you're the second coming of Jaco: If you can't fake tunes on the bandstand, you've cut yourself out of a lot of work.

How do you learn a tune on the spot and play it as if you've done it a hundred times? Do you look it up in a "fake book"—one of those telephone-book-thick volumes lead sheets to hundreds of tunes? That takes too much time—and besides, no serious player carts a stack of books to a gig. (You probably won't get to use a music stand, anyway.) Serious players use their ears. As BASS PLAYER columnist John Goldsby eloquently put it, "Bassists don't get paid to play fast—they get paid to hear fast."

Root Motion

In any chord progression, the root motion is the first thing a bassist must hear; if you don't play the proper roots, the tune will sound wrong. Ex. 1 shows several common chord movements you'll hear in all musical styles. To depict root motion we use Roman numerals that relate each root to the major-scale notes, numbered 1 through 7; chromatic roots between scale tones are shown as ♭III or ♯IV, for instance. On the CD, the examples are in the key of C. Practice these movements in all keys. I deliberately left out specific chord types so you can concentrate on each chord's root first. Later you can decide if it's major or minor, or whether it has a major or flatted 7th. (If you practice singing and playing arpeggios, you'll be better at discerning the chord quality when you get there.) Learning to think of root motion in numerical terms is a great way to pick up tunes, and it allows you to transpose instantly and hear similarities between songs.

Ex. 1

① | II V | I ‖ ② | I VI | II V ‖ ③ | I IV | V ‖ ④ | I IV | I V ‖

⑤ | I IV | III VI | II V | I ‖ ⑥ | #IV VII | III VI | II V | I ‖

⑦ | I II | III II ‖ ⑧ | I II | III bIII | II | V ‖ ⑨ | I | bVII ‖

⑩ | I | IV bVII ‖ ⑪ | I #I | II #II | III VI | II V ‖ ⑫ | I | bIII |

| bVI | bII ‖ ⑬ | I bVII | bVI V ‖ ⑭ | I III bIII | II V ‖ ⑮ | I | bVI | ⑯ | I IV |

| II V ‖ ⑰ | I III | VI | II V | I ‖ ⑱ | I | bII | ⑲ | II | V |

| III | VI ‖ ⑳ | V | I ‖ ㉑ | IV IVm | III | VI | II | V | I ‖

Harmonic Functions

Learning a song on the gig is a problem-solving exercise. The problem? "I don't know this tune!" The solution? Ears, trust, and common sense. Trust means trusting your ability to do it; if you don't believe you can, you won't. You gain musical common sense through knowledge of how chords and progressions work. A solid understanding of harmony is your best bet here. Whether you know a tune or not, understanding the natural laws of harmony will give you a sense of where a tune may go. Most songs (especially standards) follow certain patterns. This is partly why they become popular: They sound "normal" to the untrained listener.

Ex. 2 shows the diatonic and passing-chord structures for the major scale. Each structure has one of three possible functions: tonic, subdominant, or dominant. Tonic structures (Imaj7, IIIm7, VIm7) are "home bases" that start and/or end phrases. They seem to have a magnetic pull, causing other structures to want to resolve to the tonic. Dominant structures (V7, VIIm7b5, bII7, #IIdim7, #IVdim7) have a strong need to resolve to the tonic. Notice I've listed several non-diatonic dominant structures: The bII7 chord can substitute for the V7 and is commonly known as a "subV." The #IIdim7 and #IVdim7 are passing diminished chords that resolve to IIIm7 (or Imaj7/III) and Imaj7 respectively; they are dominant because they have a natural pull to tonic chords.

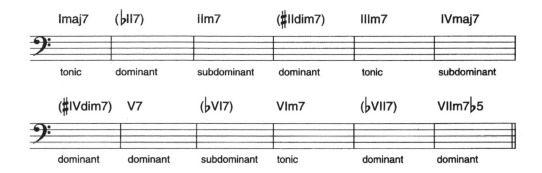

Ex. 2

Ex. 3 demonstrates some dominant resolutions. On the CD you'll hear the *C* major scale played first to establish the tonality, and then you'll hear the dominant resolution. Pay attention to the sound these resolutions create. Your ability to recognize them and find the correct root motion is crucial to your career.

Dominant Resolutions

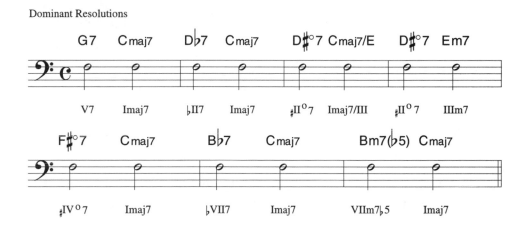

Finally, subdominant structures (IIm7, IVmaj7, ♭VI7) are used primarily to move to a dominant structure. The ♭VI7, while not diatonic to the key, is subdominant because it resolves to the V7 chord.

A classic example of harmonic function is the II–V–I cadence. The subdominant II leads to the dominant V7; the V7 in turn resolves to the tonic I (Ex. 4). This chord pattern fulfills all the harmonic functions and has a dominant root motion: II to V

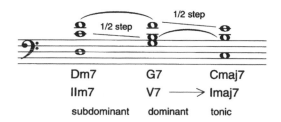

Ex. 4

is down a 5th, and V to I is down another 5th. The internal melody created by the half-step resolutions in the 3rds and 7ths (the "guide tones") further makes this pattern an essential part of Western harmony.

Learning harmony is a lifelong endeavor. There are many books available on the subject, but it's easier to grasp with the help of an experienced instructor. The above material, coupled with an ongoing ear-training program, will give you a good foundation for learning tunes on the fly.

Modulations

Many tunes visit several key centers, even though they're written in one key. This movement is called *modulation*. The most common modulation type is the pivot: A song moves along in one key and then "pivots" to a new key by using a cadence from the new key center—typically a II–V move. When a song modulates, the new key's root becomes the I for as long as it remains the tune's tonal center. A song may have a modulation built into its **A** section, but more commonly it modulates to a new key at the bridge, or **B** section. If this is the case, you'll probably have a pivotal II–V at the end of the **A** section to lead you in. You need to be able to hear these pivots and know where they lead.

Ex. 5 is a list of all the possible modulations from the I chord; they are written with the new key's II–V as the pivot. (The new key's tonal center is designated by the Roman numeral under the bracket.) On the CD the examples will be played in C. I've deliberately left out the bass part so all you will hear is the piano playing the voicings. This is all you'll get on the gig, so get used to it. It's up to you to figure out the correct root motion for each modulation. You'll need to practice these root motions in all keys, and eventually you'll learn to hear them quickly. Sometimes a pivot modulation uses only the new key's V chord, so pay attention to how the pivotal V chord relates to the original key. In the next chapter you'll have a chance to try your faking skills with the Random Modulation Torture Test.

Ex. 5

① | I | II___V → | ♭II | ② | I | II___V → | II | ③ | I | II___V → | ♭III |
          ♭II   II   ♭III

④ | I | II___V → | III | ⑤ | I | II___V → | IV | ⑥ | I | II___V → | ♯IV |
          III   IV   ♯IV

⑦ | I | II___V → | V | ⑧ | I | II___V → | ♭VI | ⑨ | I | II___V → | VI |
          V   ♭VI   VI

⑩ | I | II_____V → | ♭VII | ⑪ | I | II_____V → | VII |
          ♭VII   VII

What to Look Out for

Here are some general rules that can help you fake your way through a tune.

1. **AABA** is the most common standard-tune form. Most forms are 32 bars long, though many Cole Porter tunes are 64 bars.

2. An **A** section is usually eight bars long; if it repeats, the last measure (bar 8) will most likely set up the top of the next A with a turnaround—usually a II–V movement that sets up the next section. Common turnarounds are I–VI–II–V and III–VI–II–V (virtually the same thing).

3. The **A** section may start on the I or perhaps with a II–V–I. It may start on another chord entirely. Remember, the first chord you hear is not necessarily the tune's key.

4. The second **A** section is usually the same as the first, although its last one or two bars may be different. If the first **A** sets up the second **A** with a turnaround, often the second **A** comes to a harmonic rest point and goes to the I chord. Alternatively, the second **A** may set up the bridge with a turnaround—or perhaps does both.

5. The bridge is usually eight bars long, although sometimes it's four or 16. The most common tonal center for a bridge is the IV. The bridge usually sets up the next section with a turnaround.

6. After the bridge, the tune usually goes back to the **A** section—but not always.

7. The last **A** is usually like the second **A**, coming to a harmonic rest point at the I chord in bar 31 of a 32-bar tune. Bar 32 can be a turnaround to the top, even if it wasn't originally written that way.

Things to Practice

How do you prepare yourself for the daunting task of faking? Here's a short list:

1. Study harmony.

2. Train your ears. Be able to hear all the chromatic intervals within an octave, both ascending and descending.

3. Study chords. By sound alone, learn to identify 7, maj7, m7, m7♭5, sus7, aug7, and augmaj7 chords (to name a few).

4. Practice melody/harmony relationship drills. Go to a piano and play each of the above chord types one at a time. While the chord is ringing, play the root on

your bass, and then play each chromatic note between the root and octave. Do this slowly, and listen to what each note sounds like under each chord type.

5. Develop your pitch sense. Find a tune you can always recall, find out what key it's in, and practice hearing the tune in your head in the proper key. Practice transposing the tune to another key, and then go back to the original key.

6. Practice singing along with your bass lines.

7. Listen to records and figure out each song's key and form. Follow the arrangement and figure out the root motion while you listen.

8. Find CDs with songs you don't know, and play along. Pretend you're on the gig—in other words, no stopping!

On the Bandstand

Some things to remember when you find yourself faking your way through a tune:

1. Stay calm—you'll hear better.

2. Listen to the melody, but pay attention to *everything*.

3. Watch the piano player's left hand if possible; you may be able to see the chord progression.

4. If you're lost in the form, watch the drummer. Good drummers tend to set up the beginning of a new phrase with a fill: small fills for **A** sections, larger ones for the bridge, and something very noticeable for the top of the form.

5. Retain what you gain. If you figure out the **A** section, remember it—you'll have to play it again.

6. Say a little prayer to your deity of choice before the bridge. When you get through it, be ready to play the **A** section again.

7. Keep your eyes open—someone may signal a break in the tune.

8. Listen to what you're playing. If it sounds wrong, don't do it! If it sounds right, do it again.

9. If a certain spot is giving you trouble, remember where it is. Every time it comes up, try something else until you find a solution.

10. Construct a chord chart in your head. When the song is over, make sure to ask the name of the tune—you may have to play it again sometime.

There's a lot that goes into successful faking, so be patient. Don't back down from the challenge of learning to use your ears. Imagine the day when you'll be able to play any song that gets thrown at you, music or no music. This skill will get you more work than any amount of chops, attitude, or designer equipment. Learn to hear and make things groove, and the world will be at your feet!

▪ **Big Questions** ▪

While you are in the midst of figuring out a tune, here are some things you should ask yourself:

- What is the key?
- What is the time signature?
- What is the appropriate rhythmic feel?
- Does the feel change?
- Does this sound like anything I've heard before?
- What is the form? **AABA**, **ABAC**, **AAB**, **AB**, or **ABC**? Is it a blues?
- Does it modulate?
- What is the first chord of the **B** section?

- What material repeats?
- Are there any breaks? If so, do they happen each time through the section?
- Is the solo form the same as the melody?
- Is the melody the same on the way out as it is on the way in?
- Is there a special ending, such as a tag? (a repeated section, usually two or four measures long, played two or three times)
- Was that the end?
- Will I get hired again?

Chapter 5

Puttin' On the Tux

Wolfing down overcooked chicken clumps while the mother of the bride pesters you about getting back to the stand because it's time to throw the bouquet...smiling while the videographer does a close-up of you during the Village People medley...letting the best man sit in on drums because he used to play in a band back in college...trying to follow the bride's sister through "My Funny Valentine"...getting talked to by guests while you try to sing "Old Time Rock & Roll"....

At some point in every pro's life, the call comes for a wedding gig, a big corporate party, an anniversary dinner, a country club ball, a bowling banquet. In New England these gigs are called "GB," for general business; in New York, "club dates," for the country clubs where they often occur; in the West, "casuals," because they're usually one-shot gigs, not steady engagements.

Different names, same story: You put on a tux and play for a function. While many musicians write off these gigs as cheesy, they nonetheless pay much better than the average nightclub gig. In Boston the average pay for a four-hour casual is $200; in New York the money starts at $250; in L.A. $150. There are other advantages as well:

- Freedom. Many of these gigs require little or no commitment from players. You're there for the time hired, and that's it. No rehearsals, no lugging around the band's PA, no long-term exposure to other players' attitudes and musical shortcomings.

- Career advancement opportunities. It's surprising who you can run into on a wedding gig, especially if it's in a major city. I've played GB gigs with more than one world-renowned jazz player, and those contacts can be invaluable.

- The chance to learn new styles. In fact, you'll *have* to learn new styles, and while all might not be to your liking, your mind and repertoire will expand.

- Learning to be professional. While it's great fun to be in a club band, have a big following, get free beer, and meet members of the opposite sex, these don't always encourage a pro work ethic. But on casuals you're expected to act professionally and give the occasion the appropriate respect.

- Free food! On many casuals you can expect to be fed as part of the band's contract. Of course, this can be a mixed blessing—I've seen some horrifying things in the kitchens of those multiplex wedding factories. On the other hand, you may play at fancy hotels and get food you usually can't afford.

- New skills. These gigs can be a great place to work on such valuable tools as singing, doubling on another instrument, slapping, sight-reading, and sight-transposing.

- More money! Did I mention these gigs pay well?

The pitfalls:

- The hack factor. You'll occasionally end up playing with musicians who aren't up to your standards. When that happens, just keep repeating to yourself, *It's only four hours of my life*. And remember the money.

- The sleaze disease. You may get stuck working for an agent who holds your check for a month or two while it collects interest in *his* bank account. Before you accept any gig, make sure you settle how much and when you'll be paid.

- Stress. While these gigs are called "casuals," the client is putting out a lot of money—not only for the band but for the hall, caterers, flowers, etc. Some clients have been known to get rather, uh, excitable on the day of the big event. For you, it's just another gig; for them, it's $50,000 they didn't have to spend in the first place, and they have a way of spreading that stress around. Don't let the mother of the bride make *your* day miserable. Direct questions, comments, and problems to the bandleader. One of the reasons they get paid double is to handle these situations. Of course, some leaders will take that stress and hand it right back to you. Just keep cool, do your job, and repeat to yourself, *It's only four hours of my life*.

- Boredom. This can be deadly. If you work with the same musicians a lot you'll find yourself settling into a routine, since GB gigs tend to follow a certain format. Learning to work within the format is crucial, but if you're not careful boredom can set in. Next thing you know, you're practicing "Teen Town" during the bouquet toss. At this point you're not doing your job, and you're in danger of losing it. Remedies: Talk on breaks about playing alternate tunes, and remember there is some leeway in your own performance—if you pick your spots. While it may not be appropriate to practice Wooten-style double-thumbing during the cake-cutting ceremony, when the dance floor is full you can go for it—as long as you keep a groove. Spreading your work around with different bands is another way to keep life interesting.

- Artistic ideals. If you have lofty visions about the music business, this type of work can be a rude awakening. Face it: Playing the "Chicken Dance" at a VFW hall is a far cry from taking over the bass chair in Chick Corea's band. But you can get used to the money playing casuals, and after a while doing a $30 jazz gig doesn't seem like a great idea. If you start to feel stuck in your tux, seek out other gigs on your off time. Most casuals take place on weekends, so you'll have other nights to go out and play what you enjoy.

Make sure you cultivate a few capable substitutes, so if you get that call to fill in with Chick, you won't have to turn him down because you're booked at an Elks Club bowling banquet. A good sub is one who can do the job to the bandleader's satisfaction. If your regular group has a book of tunes, give your sub a copy in advance, along with a reference tape. If there is no book, make sure your sub is experienced enough to cut the gig without one. And plan ahead—trying to find a good sub for a Saturday night in June is like trying to find a vegetarian at a cattle ranchers' convention.

Gig Guide: Going Steady, Sitting In

GB gigs come in several forms. Here's how things work in the various scenarios:

Steady bands. In many towns most casual work goes to established groups. These vary in size and instrumentation. There may be charts ranging from simple chord sheets to specific notation and long medley arrangements. If there is no reading involved, you could be in for a lot of rehearsal, and getting a sub will be tougher. Once you've worked out your band's routine, write out a bass book to make things easier for a sub.

A band's next step is to record tunes for a demo. This can be a real eye-opener. Stay relaxed, and concentrate on playing your parts cleanly and accurately. Don't vary them too much. If you use the demo tape to make a promotional video you'll have to look like you're actually playing, and a consistent bass line will be easier to pantomime.

Steady bands often seek gigs via showcases, which usually take place in the off-season when you don't have gigs for a potential client to attend. If you work through an agency, the agent may arrange multi-band showcases at a catering hall. You'll need to wear your gig clothes and conduct yourself accordingly. You can also schedule clients to hear you at a rehearsal. You don't have to wear your tux in this situation, but you shouldn't look like a total slob.

Some steady bands have crews to cart and set up gear, but you'll likely be responsible for your own gear. You may be expected to help with the PA system, but it's not unusual for a sideman to get extra pay for doing extra duties.

When everyone in a steady group learns the roles, they can crank out the hits like a crack squad of GB commandos. This may sound mechanical, but you can get an odd sense of satisfaction when your band effortlessly segues from the Glenn Miller medley into "Love Shack."

Society gigs. This breed of casual usually occurs at fancy hotels, exclusive country clubs, or very rich people's mansions. The society orchestra is an entirely different animal from your run-of-the-mill wedding band. The bookings usually come from long-established agencies or bandleaders that have cultivated a blue-blood clientele, and they involve a different repertoire and stricter behavior codes.

The group can be anything from a trio to a 17-piece band. There is usually a book (make sure you put back the charts in order!), but a fair amount of time will be spent faking tunes. Most often, long impromptu medleys are created with tunes of similar feels. There's usually a fox-trot medley in which you'll play a two feel for days. And when I say two feel, I mean half-notes, not a tasteful melange of skips, ghost notes, and triplet pulloffs! You'll also doubtless play the half-hour-bossa-from-hell medley. ("The Girl from Ipanema" is only the beginning.)

The society bandleader will rarely tell you what the next tune is. Instead you'll get a signal in the last two bars telling you the next tune's key; two fingers pointing down means two flats (key of $B\flat$), one finger up (the index!) means one sharp (G). The key of C is usually indicated by a letter-C hand shape or a closed fist. Minor-key signals can be tricky. Some leaders signal the relative major's key signature, so a two-flat sign could mean G minor. Other leaders signal G minor by giving the two-flat sign and then sticking a finger sideways to indicate a minus sign. To make things more confusing, some leaders use fingers-up for flat keys and fingers-down for sharp, probably because flat keys are more common and it's easier to point up than down.

When you get the signal, play a quick IIm–V in the last bar of the tune to go into the new key, and be prepared to scramble if the new tune doesn't start on the I chord. When you get good at this you'll learn tunes' standard keys and even be able to guess the next song from the key signal. If you're backing a singer, be prepared to play in weird keys. If, for instance, you get thrown off playing "Stella by Starlight" in *G* instead of *B♭*, use your ears, watch the piano player's left hand, and relax.

Medleys can be a real test of your tune knowledge; it's not uncommon to cover 15 tunes in one medley. In addition to knowing the usual standards, society bassists should learn the stock big-band arrangements for "In the Mood," "String of Pearls," and "Moonlight Serenade"—you *will* play them.

Society musicians are expected to behave with decorum: no hanging around the hors d'oeuvre table like a flock of vultures, no rushing the bar on breaks, and no telling dirty jokes near a live microphone. If a break room is provided, use it.

Sub gigs. You may get called to sub with an established band. In this kind of gig the challenges include reading the book (if there is one), locking in with the drummer, keeping eye contact with the leader, resisting the urge to overplay, playing at an appropriate volume, using your ears and common sense, and getting along with the other musicians.

Pickup bands. These gigs can be heaven or hell—or both. Free from the rigidity of a set band, a group of savvy GB mercenaries can do a great job and have lots of fun. But you can also get stuck fulfilling the ever-present request to "play some Stones!" with a trumpet/accordion/drum-machine combo. In either case, you need to be ready for anything. This means reading all types of charts, knowing tons of tunes—everything from Benny Goodman to the Spice Girls—knowing the typical wedding shtick (cake-cutting, garter-belt ritual, bouquet toss, ethnic tunes), having quick ears, following the leader's cues, and knowing the right style for any given tune.

GB ABCs

Some tips that will make your casual work easier and help you get gigs:

- Have decent-looking clothes: tux for men, black formal for women. Wearing a tux for three gigs a weekend all season long takes its toll. Don't leave that deviled-egg stain on the lapel—get it cleaned! You'll be on your feet a lot, so find a pair of comfortable black shoes. (Only drummers can get away with wearing black sneakers.) And carry a spare bow tie.

- Never pay retail for a tux. All formal-wear shops sell off their rental stock. Professional discounts aren't uncommon, so tell the tux shop if you play with an established band or through a well-known agency.

- Make sure you have clear directions to the gig, and show up in enough time to set up. Being late is a sure way to lose a gig.

- Bring an appropriate amp. Ask about the size of the room. Some places have horrendous load-ins, so travel light, but not too light.

- Be inconspicuous. If you don't know where to load in, drive around to the back of the hall. You'll probably see other band members' cars. Don't assume you can load in through the front door.

- Arrive dressed for the gig, unless you're setting up well before guests show up.

- Check your attitude at the door. You may be hot stuff, but what counts on the gig is your willingness to cooperate and get along.

- Try to smile. Many potential gigs have been lost because the band looked glum. Keep the vibe light by discreetly telling jokes onstage. And remember: You can always raise a smile by pondering the absurdity of a room full of otherwise intelligent people doing the Hokey Pokey.

- Play solid, appropriate lines; showing off your chops is not what you're getting paid for.

- Learn tunes and develop your ears! The player with the best ears and the biggest repertoire usually gets the gig. Listen to Top 40 radio; you'll have to play a lot of those tunes.

By now you should be well prepared to venture into the lucrative world of casual gigs. So keep your attitude straight, your tux pressed, and—by the way—are you working New Year's Eve?

The Random Modulation Torture Test

This example is designed to give you a small glimpse of the listening skills you'll need to survive a pickup society gig. Endless medleys are the rule, and modulations can come at the end of each chorus. This exercise is a I–VI–II–V vamp played as a bossa nova (one bar per chord change). It starts in C but modulates every four bars. In bar 4 of each key, you'll hear a pivot modulation to the new key on beats *three* and *four*, so in a sense, this is really a I–VI–II–V/pivot II–V progression.

TRACK
31

▪ Name That Tune—And Learn It! ▪

Amazing as it may seem, this list shows only a fraction of the songs you need to learn to be a fully armed GB warrior. Ask friends who do casual gigs what tunes they play, and get copies of their song lists if possible. There are several fake books that contain tunes for weddings and other functions; just remember that on the gig you won't have time to look up a tune.

Each region has its own requirements. The ethnic groups represented in your town will affect what specialty tunes you need to know. In New York City you may not have to know all of the country hits; in Nashville you will. Current pop songs are important everywhere.

Rock, R&B

Blue Suede Shoes; Brown Eyed Girl; Chain of Fools; Heard It Through the Grapevine; I Can't Help Myself (Sugar Pie, Honey Bunch); I Got You (I Feel Good); In the Midnight Hour; Jailhouse Rock; Johnny B. Goode; Kansas City; Knock on Wood; Louie Louie; Mony Mony; Mustang Sally; My Girl; Old Time Rock & Roll; Proud Mary; Respect; Rock Around the Clock; Rockin' Robin; Shout; Soul Man; Twist & Shout; Wooly Bully; You Can't Hurry Love

Swing Standards

All of Me; All the Things You Are; Autumn Leaves; Body and Soul; Darn That Dream; Don't Get Around Much Anymore; Fly Me to the Moon (In Other Words); Gone with the Wind; If I Were a Bell; I Love You; In the Mood; Jersey Bounce; Misty; Moonlight in Vermont; Moonlight Serenade; More (Theme from *Mondo Cane*); My Romance; New York, New York; Our Love Is Here to Stay; Pennsylvania 6-5000; Polka Dots &

Moonbeams; Satin Doll; Skylark; Stardust; Stompin' at the Savoy; String of Pearls; Take the "A" Train; Tenderly; These Foolish Things (Remind Me of You); They Can't Take That Away from Me; What's New

Bossa Novas

Blue Bossa; Corcovado (Quiet Nights of Quiet Stars); A Day in the Life of a Fool; Desafinado; Dindi; The Girl from Ipanema; If You Never Come to Me; Meditation; Once I Loved; Samba de Orfeu; Summer Samba; Triste; Watch What Happens (Lola's Theme); Wave

Pop Standards

Achy Breaky Heart; Boogie Oogie Oogie; Breezin'; Caught Up in the Rapture; Celebration; Crazy; Disco Inferno; The Electric Slide; The Hustle; I Will Always Love You; Last Dance; Love Shack; Macarena; Mercy Mercy; Morning Dance; Party Train; Pink Cadillac; Rhythm Is Gonna Get Ya; Roll with It; The Rose; Saving All My Love for You; Songbird; Sunny; Sweet Love; That's All I Ask of You; Unchained Melody; Unforgettable; We've Only Just Begun; The Wind Beneath My Wings; Winelight; Y.M.C.A.

Ethnic & Specialty Tunes

Alley Cat; Beer Barrel Polka; Cella Luna; The Chicken Dance; Danny Boy; Dansero; El Cumbanchero; The Farmer in the Dell (The Bride Cuts the Cake); Hava Nagila; The Hokey Pokey; La Bamba; Lichtensteiner Polka; Never on a Sunday; Pennsylvania Polka; Quando Quando Quando; Sabor a' Mi; Simon Tov; The Stripper; Sunrise Sunset; Tarentella; Tea for Two; Too Fat Polka; When Irish Eyes Are Smiling

■ A Tale of Two Cities ■

How do tux gigs compare in the nation's two biggest music markets? To find out we asked a pair of busy bassists in New York and Los Angeles. Our East Coast man was Steve Marks, a Bass Collective teacher, freelancer, and author of *Developing Reading Skills for the Contemporary Bassist* and *The Zen of Bass* [$16 each from Box 20653, Cherokee Station, NY 10021].

"This is a typical New York club date: It's Saturday night, you're in the Grand Ballroom of the Waldorf or maybe some country club in the 'burbs. You rush in from playing the cocktail hour—usually the best part of the gig—set up and are ready to play in the time it takes a rabbit to sneeze. The band is playing either "Celebration" or a bouncy swing tune. For the next four hours you've got disco, current Top 40 (especially ballads and novelty numbers), oldies, rumbas, waltzes, cha-chas, swing, inane line dances, ethnic tunes, and Motown. You're expected to know every song ever written in every key, even if you're subbing. When leaders really want to torture you they don't tell you the next tune; they just use hand signals to indicate the key.

"If the leader is scowling, it doesn't necessarily mean he hates you. He's probably burned out from ten or 15 years of this. There used to be a lot more freelance work, but now it's mostly set groups. For your five hours of bass services you'll receive around $250; afternoons and weekdays pay about $50 less. If your band is a cooperative you might make more. Getting gigs is usually by word of mouth, although I've seen audition notices in the newspaper. The top bands play 150 or more jobs a year. Nobody cares much what equipment you use as long as it sounds decent and is reliable. Having a reliable car is also essential.

"The gigs don't always suck. New York's pool of musicians is tremendous, and you're often gigging alongside kick-ass players. Occasionally the music ignites."

Providing the West Coast perspective is Bruce Stone. His TV and film credits include *The Byron Allen Show, Married...with Children, Ghost Dad,* and *The Naked Truth.* You can also hear him on jingles for Reebok and the NBA, and on albums by keyboardist Keiko Matsui, trumpeter Tony Guerrero, and others. He has performed with such artists as guitarist Larry Coryell, bassist Brian Bromberg, flutist Dave Valentin, and sax men Ernie Watts and Gerald Albright.

"In L.A. the last five years the industry has changed dramatically because of sampling, and a lot of guys who would be doing only session work are now doing casuals as well. The money usually starts at $150 and goes up according to your skills, how much the leader likes you, and if you sing. Vocals put you much more in demand.

"The level of players on these gigs is scary. The big offices hire a lot of people who have done major tours, so if you work with those bands, it isn't unusual to get a referral to a major act. It can also lead to studio calls.

"Most of the L.A. booking offices hire freelance players instead of set bands. Most of the time clients are buying the bandleader and vocalist—people understand that bands change all the time. When I decided to do less road work and more casuals, I got together a résumé, a photo, and a list of my vocal tunes, and sent it to all the major L.A. agencies. If you do that sooner or later someone will call you as a last-minute fill-in. Referrals also play a part in getting gigs. If you know someone in the industry, they can recommend you to an agency. For one of the offices, I did a video playing upright bass and looking rather animated; that has sold me a number of times because people like that look. Getting your first shot isn't that hard, but staying there is the trick."

Chapter 6

Jazz Survival

You've spent considerable time and energy studying jazz. You've devoured a few books on walking bass lines and soloing; you are continually improving your time, feel, and groove with consistent and focused metronome work; you are spending lots of time doing the required listening; and you've studied with your local jazz guru. Now you're ready to hit the scene—you're ready to gig, right?

Almost. There are still quite a few things you'll need to know to function properly in a jazz context. Some of these skills are learned on the gig by trial and error. Because jazz is spontaneous, it's impossible to be 100% prepared for everything. Jazz, much like life, will throw you a curve just when you think you've got it all together. Some of the things you'll need to know are simple—yet if you are unaware of them, they can become a problem on the bandstand. Some are the little tricks all experienced players know but never discuss. Some you may just feel too foolish to ask about. Let's face it: Jazz musicians place a certain amount of value on being hip—and if you ain't hip, it can be a real drag, dig? So let's get hip to some timely tips and learn some important jazz survival skills.

Form

As a bassist your primary responsibilities are to keep the time flow happening, to outline the chord changes with interesting lines, and—extremely important—to keep the tune's form intact. Sure, we all play some notes that are questionable at times, and we may even speed up or slow down a little now and then. While these sins may be deplorable, they are forgivable. Screwing up the form, however, is like wearing a Greenpeace T-shirt at a loggers convention—a big mistake. Unfortunately, you will screw up the form at some time or another; it happens to all beginning jazz bassists. But as you become more familiar with the tunes, you will be able to keep your place. And with experience, you will see it's possible to find your way back without anyone noticing you were lost. Here's how:

- **Relax.** If you panic about being lost, it's much harder to get back on track.

- **Listen.** There are many cues being played that will help you find your way. Drum fills most often happen at the end of four- or eight-bar phrases, bigger ones lead in or out of the bridge (if there is one), and most drummers do something to set up the top of the form. Examine the changes (if you have them in front of you), and look for landmarks. For instance, in a 12-bar blues, the IV chord is a landmark. The V chord (or the II–V) is another landmark. Being able to hear these changes will tell you where you are. In "Rhythm" changes, the big landmark is the bridge. The **A** sections are usually in the key of *B♭*, but when the bridge hits, you may have an *F♯* from the *D7* chord smacking you in the face. You need to be able to hear that note.

- **Keep your eyes open.** Many players close their eyes when they get deep into a jazz trance. That's fine, but if you get lost and can't hear your way out, open your eyes and look around. Usually someone will be willing to help you out. However, in the Big City approach to learning jazz, sometimes the attitude is "sink or swim." In many cases, people will ignore you just to teach you a lesson—and you *will* learn it.

- **Don't stop playing.** The bassist's primary obligations are (1) to keep the pulse, (2) to keep the form, and (3) to create harmonically and rhythmically relevant lines. If you lose the form, you've blown #2, and #3 is no longer possible—but #1 still has a chance if you keep plowing through. Keep playing strongly, even if the notes are all wrong. It's better to be partially right than totally wrong—which is what you'll be if you stop. While you continue to play, relax, listen, and keep your eyes open, and you'll find your place again.

By the way, the best way to learn to keep your place in a tune is to learn its melody. Find a recording of the tune, and practice singing the melody to yourself while the soloists play.

Performance Protocol

Jazz groups have a performance protocol to ensure things run smoothly. Each player is responsible for understanding how the group functions as well as his or her instrument's role within it. While some groups search for new approaches to the jazz format, most use the standard format. Knowing this information enables players who have never met to get together and make music.

There are many variations, but the most basic jazz-tune format is: intro, head (melody), solos, head, and out (ending). Listen to jazz recordings and identify the events that take place from start to finish.

Intros

The intro may consist of material from the tune about to be played, or it may be a simple pedal point on the 5th of the key. In some cases the intro may be a miniature composition of its own, as in the famous intro to Charlie Parker's version of "All the Things You Are." You can hear it on *Charlie Parker Jam Session* [Verve].

A common intro device is the "vamp," often used when players segue from one tune to another (a regular practice on society gigs). A vamp is a short progression that repeats until someone gives a cue to move on to the next section—in this case, the head. The most common vamp is the I–VI–II–V progression in the same key as the tune to be played. A common variation is III–VI–II–V; this vamp works well if the tune's first chord is the I. If a song starts on the II chord, the vamp will usually end with a II–V leading to the II chord. Intros are most often four or eight bars long, depending on the tune's tempo. For a slow tune, eight bars will feel too long; for a ballad, two may be enough.

Another common intro is the dominant pedal. The dominant is the 5th of the key—so in *B♭*, the dominant pedal is *F*. The most popular way of using this intro is to play the pedal on beats *two* and *four*; this is referred to as "pedal on the V, *two* and *four*" (Ex. 1). Notice how in bar 4 there's a little skip on beat *four*; it helps get the momentum going for the head.

Ex. 1

Sometimes the dominant pedal will have a rhythmic figure or "kick" everyone plays. Again, we set up the head with an approach note to get things moving (Ex. 2).

Ex. 2

You can also sustain the pedal point with long tones (Ex. 3). Notice we start to walk a bit earlier here. After sitting on the sustained pedal, it takes a little more time to get the momentum going. This is just one way to do it. You don't have to set up the head—you can just start walking on beat one.

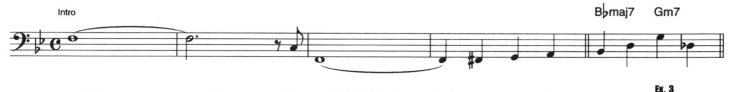

Ex. 3

One more common intro uses the tune's last four or eight bars to set up the top. This is called "last four" or "last eight."

Endings

Most of the time, everyone starts playing a tune without any idea of how to end it. But remember—most listeners can recall a tune's beginning and ending, but they forget much of what happens in between. So if your intro is sloppy and the ending a train wreck, people will think your band is lousy. Of course, there will be some listeners who can appreciate the brilliant improvisation that comes in between—but to be safe, you should have some "stock" endings under your fingers.

Ex. 4 is the all-time classic, No. 1 stock ending. It's old, but it works every time. This one has many subtle variations; sometimes there's a "stinger" on beat *four* of the last bar, and sometimes you may extend it with the kicks shown in Ex. 5.

Ex. 4

Ex. 5

Ex. 6 is a variation using the basic rhythmic idea, but it avoids the cliché of the actual line. It works well because everyone can play the obvious rhythmic kicks while the horn players or pianist improvise an ending.

Ex. 6

Ex. 7 is called the "Basie" ending (as in Count Basie). The bass leaves a hole for the signature piano lick, hitting the "bump" on beat *four*.

Ex. 7

Ex. 8's slightly extended ending shown uses a descending chromatic progression from the ♯IVm7♭5 chord; it's called the "♯IV" ending. The rhythmic kicks are optional. Sometimes players extend the ♯IV ending by giving each chord a full measure.

Ex. 8

Some tunes' melodies may have built-in rhythmic kicks you can use as an ending. Look at how the melody ends—it may be a convenient way to get out of the tune. Another common practice is the "triple tag," in which you repeat the tune's last two bars three times. There's also the "vamp" ending, which extends itself with a III–VI–II–V progression; it can go on for days until someone takes the lead and cues an ending.

Solos

After you've played the intro and the head (once if it's a long form, twice if it's short), next come the solos. While there are many possible solo-section configurations, the default hierarchy is: horns, piano (and/or other comping instrument), bass, drums. However, drums are not always last, and the bass and drums do not necessarily solo on every tune. For some reason, musicians often assume you don't want to solo on "Moment's Notice" at 300 bpm—but if you want to, make eye contact so someone doesn't jump ahead to the drums or the head.

During solos pay attention to each player's approach. Is the soloist playing "inside" or "outside"? Aggressively or relaxed? Building ideas or spewing out licks? All of these influence how you back them up. In jams, players sometimes forget themselves and play past the point of common courtesy. Are they playing too long? It's sometimes appropriate to drop a musical "hint"—for instance, going to a sustained pedal tone in the form's last two bars. I've been known to give someone two or three hints and then just drop out completely, leaving them alone with the drums—that's usually their last chorus! (But don't give a "hint" to the person who hired you.)

Drum solos are handled in a few ways. Sometimes the drummer takes a "chorus," which is a solo on the tune's entire form. Here's where it's important to know the melody. To keep your place in the form during the drum solo, sing the melody to yourself. (Let's hope the drummer knows the melody, too.) Another drum-solo option is "trading fours" or "trading eights"—swapping four- or eight-bar phrases with the drums. After the bass solo, start at the top and walk for four or eight bars, and then stop while the drummer takes his turn. Stay focused here; some drummers like to get crafty and phrase things in unusual ways. If you aren't paying attention, you may come in wrong—sometimes with disastrous results. Focus on the hi-hat. Drummers often keep it going on beats *two* and *four* throughout their trading. If you don't hear the hi-hat, count whole notes. Some drummers occasionally stretch their two bars a little—or even shrink them. If you are following along, it may be obvious where your drummer intends to land—so you'll have to just go with him in order to keep it happening.

Sitting In

If you're new in town or just getting into the scene, you'll need to sit in at a club. Sitting in will get you in touch with other players, get you heard in public, and (we hope) get you a gig somewhere. There may or may not be places to do this where you live; search out the jazz gigs in the newspaper's club listings. Even if a particular gig is not a jam session, you may be allowed to sit in. Call ahead or ask around about what type of place it is; you don't want to go into a fancy supper club looking like a Butthole Surfers roadie. Don't gripe if you have to pay a cover charge—it usually goes to the band, and it might be your salary one day. Remember that in a club you're expected to spend some cash. You don't have to drink alcohol (you're better off if you don't), but buy *something*—a soda or some juice, and more than one drink—and tip well. In addition to being common courtesy, it's good politics. You may gig in that place someday, and you can be sure the staff will remember you if you stiff them! And the bartender could be in charge of booking the bands.

Musical manners. Once you settle in, check out the scene. If it's a jam session, there may be a sign-up list. If not, you'll have to do some schmoozing. Approach the bassist during the break and tell him you'd like to play. If it's not a jam session, you should politely inquire about the sitting-in policy. It's not acceptable everywhere, and if the musicians don't know you, you may be met with some reluctance. If so, don't push it—it may not be the bassist's decision, and you'll want to remain on good terms with him. He may want to talk to you a little to see if you know what's what. Be honest. Don't tell him you just got back from Europe with Joe Henderson if in fact you just finished your first semester at music school. At the same time, don't sound down on yourself; people will assume it's for a good reason. Just be real.

Let's say you get to sit in. If you play electric you should bring your own bass, but you'll likely be allowed to use the house amp. Be respectful—don't make major EQ changes without asking permission, and put the controls back when you're done. Also, don't crank the volume; if you've been hearing the house bassist fine, leave the volume knob alone.

If you play upright be prepared to play the house bassist's instrument. Playing someone else's upright can be a tough experience—but that's life in the Big City. When you watch the house band play, pay careful attention to how the bassist plays. It may give you important clues about how to approach that particular instrument.

Instruments can get extreme—I once ended up sitting in on jazz monster Ratzo Harris's 6-string upright, which was definitely not a comfortable situation. But even an unfamiliar 4-string can throw you off if you let it. First, relax. Then check out the action. Are the strings three inches off the fingerboard, or are they sitting nearly right on it? The key is find a way to swing and be creative with the bass you're playing. If the action is low, don't try to dig in like Charles Mingus on an angry day. If it's really high, don't worry about showing off your Eddie Gomez thumb-position licks. Once you're on the bandstand, all you have to do is sound good.

Different drummers. In addition to possibly playing someone else's axe, you'll be working with an unfamiliar drummer. Before you start, observe the house drummer's style closely and try to place the influences. Elvin? Tony? DeJohnette? Blakey? Buddy? Understanding these styles' differences will help you hook up with more drummers. If you're lucky you'll get to play with the drummer you've been watching; otherwise you'll play with someone who's also sitting in. That could be good or bad. Even if they play well, they're not warmed up, they're stepping into unfamiliar ground, and they might be a little nervous—just like you. Whatever the case, if the drummer and you are meeting for the first time, be sure to make eye contact before you start playing. Then lay it down the best you can, and see if the drummer is at least on the same planet as you. If you feel the tempo pushing or pulling, try to figure out the source of the problem. It might be you. Always be willing to adjust your groove to connect with the drummer. He may not be as flexible as you are, but it's important you both sound good. If you can learn to swing with any drumming style, you'll be able to jump confidently into any situation and make it work.

Two worlds. There are two basic types of sitting-in experience. One is friendly and relaxed: Everyone is pleasant and willing to help you feel comfortable. They may let you call some tunes, and they might have a fake book you can read from. They also may not get upset if you don't play like a top professional. This is your chance to learn valuable lessons with more-experienced players. If you are a new player or slightly shy about sitting in, look for these situations—it's a good way to get some experience.

The other situation is the Big City experience: There are two bass players ahead of you, and both are heavy pros. There is a line of about 15 tenor players against the wall, all ready to take their 25 choruses apiece—not to mention the four trumpet players, two trombone players, and a guitarist. The pianist doesn't look you in the eye, and the drummer gives you a sideways glance that says, "Who the hell is this clown?" You settle into the bass spot, which is crammed between the piano and the constantly opening restroom door. You play some open strings to check the feel...hmm, the action's a little high. A horn player steps up and calls a tune. Everyone else seems to know it, but you don't. A lump forms in your throat, and before you can say anything, you hear the sax player say "*D♭*" and then count off the tune at 300 BPM. That's when you notice that the house bassist has put his amp on standby.

To survive in this poisonous environment, you'd better have nerves of steel, have your time together, know the performance protocol and lots of tunes, have big ears and be an ace at faking, and groove like a Lincoln doing 85 on the interstate. And make it look like you do it all every day.

Out chorus. Let's assume you did survive. In fact, you did great. Now what? Once you've proven yourself, people will lighten up a little—but if you're in New York or another major town, don't expect folks to fall at your feet. Your survival is not a big deal to them—it's an *expectation*. If you get a compliment, don't immediately start making excuses about why you didn't sound as good as you could—just say "thank you" and perhaps say something nice about the bass. Make sure you have your business cards with you. Phone numbers written on a cocktail napkin usually get used to blow someone's nose. Once you start to prove yourself, get to know the other bass players; they'll need subs and will be able to help you the most.

Remember you get only one chance to make a first impression, so it's essential to be prepared. Take your time, do your homework, and stay in the background for a while to check out what's happening. When you find a place you think you can handle, go for it—and swing hard!

Chapter 7

Freelancing: Nine Steps to Nailing the Gig

We enjoy a unique position in the musical food chain. Every band needs a bass player, and there are never enough of us to go around. That gives you lots of opportunities for freelancing. Rather than lock in with one band, you can play a wide variety of musical styles with several groups—all in one week.

There are many skills and tools you need to be a successful freelancer: good time, common-sense music theory knowledge, reading ability, quick ears, a wide range of musical techniques, knowledge of various styles, the uncanny ability to play what is appropriate in any given situation, reliable and versatile equipment, good people skills, time-management skills, a decent-running car....

As a freelancer you can enjoy a charmed life. (When you're working, anyway.) You gig with a band, save the day, receive lots of strokes for doing a great job, get paid, and leave—all without having to load up the PA. Of course, there's no roadie to help you carry your SVT, and you may never wind up on MTV. But you can make a good living playing bass, establish a reputation as an individual player, have many satisfying musical experiences, and never have to work a day job.

Step One: Keep Time

There are several conflicting opinions on how to develop good time—but you *must* have it. It's at the core of everything we do as bassists. So how do you develop good time? My answer is to use a metronome. Chapter 1, Keeping Time, tells you how.

The goal of freelancing is to make the people who hire you happy. You'll often work as a substitute with an existing band. In these cases you'll find they've developed a group sense of time and groove. It's your job to fit in with these players, not to force them to undergo major changes for a one-nighter. If you find a way to groove with them, they'll be happy—even if they have time problems. When your time is strong, you can help smooth out trouble spots. And if the band is already solid, they'll really like you.

Step Two: Know Your Music

A good base of musical knowledge is essential if you want to take any freelance call that comes in. You *must* be able to read music. Not every gig will require it, but you never know when someone is going to pull out a chart and expect you to follow it. Reading means dealing with specific written notation as well as chord charts. If you need to get your reading together, check out my October '96 BASS PLAYER article, "Sight-Reading Methods & Materials," which looks at many excellent books to help you toward musical literacy. Chart reading is a separate skill; it entails reading notation plus making sense out of chord symbols. For help on that subject, refer to Chapter 2, Navigating a Chord Chart. If you live in Nashville, you'll need to know the Nashville number system, which was detailed in David Hungate's "Nashville Notes" column in the March '95 BASS PLAYER and is also available on the Web at **www.bassplayer.com/trenches**.

In addition to reading, you should know the numerical shorthand system for referring to chord progressions. By representing the major scale's notes with the numbers one through eight (written as Roman numerals), the system helps you learn root motions and chord progressions quickly—even while the guitarist is screaming them to you from across the stage. (Ex. 1; scale degree VIII is always called "I.")

Ex. 1

I   II   III   IV   V   VI   VII   VIII

You will need to know all the basic chord types and scales, as well as how to use them. You must have a complete knowledge of the fingerboard. Joe Hubbard introduced a good neck-learning exercise in the March/April '91 BASS PLAYER; essentially, you start on low *E* and play every *E* up and down the neck. Then you go to *F* and repeat. Do this with each note, and eventually you'll know the entire fingerboard. You also have to know the names of the notes in each key; if someone tells you to play I–VI–II–V in *G*, you have to know what the corresponding root notes are. You can get away with learning only the fingerboard patterns, but gaps in your understanding will limit your earning power.

Learn your key signatures, too. You need to know how many sharps or flats each key has, because it's common for a bandleader to indicate the key just by saying "two flats" or "three sharps." As we discussed in the previous chapter, it's also common to use fingers to signal the key. In most places, fingers held up means sharp keys, while fingers down means flats—but make sure you know the local convention. In Boston, for instance, fingers up means flat keys—so three fingers up would mean the song is in the key of E♭. In Providence, only 45 miles away, fingers up means sharp keys; in that case, three fingers up would indicate the key of *A*.

To learn key signatures, study Ex. 2, which shows the circle of 5ths. *C* is at the 12 o'clock position with no sharps or flats. The sharp keys appear in order starting clockwise, and the flat keys start counterclockwise.

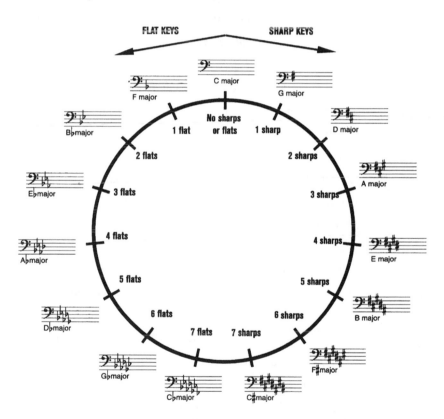

Ex. 2

Step Three: Know Different Kinds of Music

Being a freelancer requires you to be familiar with many different styles of music. Even if you're into only one style, with a little common sense and an open mind, you can play just about anything. When something different comes on the radio, don't change the station; check it out. Listen to the bass line. What do you hear? From one style to another, bass lines are made up of similar elements. Roots, 5ths, and octaves;

outlining the root motion; hooking up with the drum part; and creating fills that enhance the feel are universal ingredients of good bass lines. Of course, you'll need some specialized technical requirements, even if you don't become an expert. For example, people usually expect you to be able to slap, so you should be at least pass- able at the technique. Conversely, if you're a slap player, have the brains to know when *not* to slap! Few things are more obnoxious than someone turning every song into a pseudo-funk tune.

Playing bass chords isn't usually called for—but if the keyboard shuts down or if the guitarist doesn't know the tune, playing chords can save the day. Check out Chapter 11 for the basic technique. The thumb-mute technique discussed in Chap- ter 10 can also help you to fit in by simulating an old-style acoustic bass sound. (Use it the next time you have to play "Fly Me to the Moon," and watch the old- timers smile.) It can also help you to get a deeper bass sound for styles such as reg- gae and blues.

Tapping can be another way to hold things together when the guitar player is late or the keyboardist's rack blows a fuse. And, of course, the next time you get a call for a metal-fusion gig, you'll be all set. Just remember: If you take a country gig, leave your tapping chops at home!

One of the biggest stumbling blocks bass players face is repertoire. Many times I've needed a sub and had to pass over a great player because he didn't know tunes. Many situations (especially pickup bands) require you to come to the gig ready to play anything—'40s standards, '50s rock & roll, '60s R&B, '70s disco, '80s new wave, '90s alternative. There may be no charts, and you may have to make quick segues to keep the dance floor moving. How do you do that? Listen to all styles of music and absorb what you hear. Also, *play* different styles, and notice recurring elements. Learn to recognize common root motions, and check out the root motion exercise in Chapter 4. Of course, if your ears are together, you'll be able to fake through the tune the first time and have it nailed by the repeat. Ex. 3 is a "Style-O-Rama" vamp. The progression is a basic I-VI-II-V vamp in C major, but the style changes every eight bars. The order is bossa, half-time funk, swing, country, reggae, rumba, swing two-feel, eighth-note rock, Motown.

Ex. 3

Listen closely to how the bass part changes for the various rhythmic styles. Also notice how some things stay the same. The root of each chord is always played on beat *one*, a universal truth for functional bass playing.

Most often, you'll be called upon to play solid, no-nonsense bass. Be prepared to do that, and you'll have no problems. If you are unfamiliar with a style or a tune, use common sense: Less is more. Listen to the melody, listen to the changes, and listen to the drums. Which brings us to the next requirement for being a successful freelancer: ears.

Step Four: Listen

Quick ears are essential for freelancers—you need to be able to hear something and immediately play the right thing. If you work on the ear training program I prescribed in Chapter 3, you will be well on your way to having your ears together.

Step Five: Get Equipped

Let's assume you have your chops together, your ears are in shape, and you know the tunes. That's it, right? No, you'll also need some specific items to freelance successfully. You should have reliable, versatile equipment. This could mean several choices of instruments, or just one all-purpose axe. A fretless is good for special circumstances. If you have multiple axes, make sure the right one is in your gig bag before you leave for work. You should have at least two good working amps—including a head of at least 200 watts—and a choice of cabinets. My cabinet preference is a 2x10 + tweeter and a 4x10 + tweeter; this gives me several options, depending on the size of the room I need to cover. I also recommend a good-sounding combo amp to help you get in and out of the gig quickly. When you're faced with the infamous "load-in from hell," you'll happily walk through the front door discreetly carrying your 15" combo while the keyboard player waits next to the dumpster for the security guard to open the loading dock. Make sure you carry an extra set of strings, a tuner, a strap, a good instrument cable, an extension cord (a 10' household cord will save you), a spare battery if you use an active bass, and an all-purpose tool for emergency adjustments. If you want to be a real Boy Scout, carry a power strip, a music stand, a portable soldering iron, extra cables, a spare power cord for your amp, and—the thing that keeps America running—duct tape. And if you want to make instant friends of forgetful bandmates, carry guitar picks and a drum key.

It's also important to have a reliable car. Although bass players are enough in demand that you can mooch rides, do you really want to wait for the drummer to break down his hardware, help him carry it, and then have to listen to his Buddy Rich tapes all the way home? Make sure your car will get you there; the last thing you need is to be stuck on the interstate when the band is due to play the Motown medley. Be punctual: Leave yourself enough time to run into traffic, get lost, and set up your gear. It doesn't matter how good you are, if you consistently show up late, you won't get called back. (Hint: If the first thing you see when you walk in is the bandleader taking his nitro pill, you're cutting it too close.)

Step Six: Get Organized

Time management is paramount. Get a date book and write things down. Don't take a gig unless you can check the book and be *sure* you are free. Double-booking yourself occasionally happens—but it's better to know far in advance. You don't want to spend Saturday afternoon scrambling to find a bass player to cover your gig that night. If you go for a "double"—two gigs in one day—make sure you have enough time to get from one to the next. You may have to drive long distances, switch over your gear, change your clothes, and eat. This is where having two rigs comes in handy; if necessary, you can have one amp set up and waiting for you at your second gig.

Once you get busy, choose your gigs wisely. If you take care of business, at some point you'll have your pick of many opportunities. Don't take a gig if you're sure something better will show up. Rather than commit four months in advance to a $50 Saturday night, you may want to wait—if you later get a call for a $200 gig the same night, you'll kick yourself. In that case, whatever you do, don't call the leader of the first gig the day before to tell him you can't make it. You're better off losing the extra money than getting a reputation for being unreliable. If you need to get out of a gig for some reason, find your own sub—someone the leader approves. If your sub can't cut the gig, it's a reflection on you—and you will hear about it the next time you work with that band—if there *is* a next time.

Step Seven: Think Green

When someone calls about a gig, don't be shy about asking how much you will get paid; after all, it's business. Before you say you are available, ask for details while you "look for your book." Ask who, what, when, where, what you need to wear, etc.

With this knowledge you can decide if you want to take the job. If it meets your criteria, you can finally "find" your book and check the date. Don't take a gig without finding out about money first, because you don't want to be surprised at the end of the night. Of course, when you work for the same clients all the time, you develop a trust that the money will be what you expect. But whatever you do, don't be snooty about money. If the "bread is short," just say no. If you feel compelled to mention that the money isn't enough, do it tactfully and with respect; you might trigger a better offer.

Step Eight: Know Your Place

When you show up for the gig (on time), ask the leader if there's a preference about where you set up. If there's a "book" for the gig, stand next to the keyboardist or guitarist if possible. They can guide you through tough spots, and you can look on with them if they're using the book, too. Set up your amp close to the drummer; if he has to strain to hear you from behind the guitar rig, you both may have a hard time nailing the groove. If you're playing with a band for the first time, say hello, be polite and friendly, and avoid copping an attitude. In general, develop a relaxed, professional demeanor. Even if the band is not very talented, it may still be a source of income. If you can't stand playing with them, there's no need to alienate anyone; the next time they call, just politely say you're booked. Don't be a jerk—keep your gig karma clean! Remember: Even the lamest gig can lead to a referral for a great one.

Step Nine: Look the Part

Make sure you dress properly. You don't want to wear a tuxedo to a Steppenwolf tribute gig at the local biker bar, and you don't want to stroll into the Ritz-Carlton wearing a tank top. If you're going to freelance for a living, you should buy your own tux. Keep it fairly clean. (I always get mine cleaned once a year, even if it doesn't need it.) Have a few shirts and a spare bow tie. Get comfortable black shoes (not black sneakers) and black socks. You'll need something to wear for "suit" and "jacket-and-tie" gigs; a black suit is all-purpose. The standard country-club outfit is a navy-blue blazer, white shirt, and gray pants. It's good to have some "real" pants (not blue jeans) and nice shirts for "dressy casual" gigs. You may want to have some regional clothes as well; for instance, if you're playing a casual in south Florida, study a Jimmy Buffett album cover. I live in Tucson, where boots and a cowboy hat can come in handy. (So far I haven't needed the hat.) Another fashion tip: Black jeans are very versatile.

It may seem silly to devote so much attention to your wardrobe—but don't forget, people are looking at you as well as listening to you. Most likely, they understand what they see better than what they hear.

When it comes to making it as a freelancer, remember that at a certain level, tons of people have the chops to do the gig. The calls will come to you because of your reputation for taking care of business, whatever the gig. Good luck—and if you need a sub, give me a call!

Section
Three

Specialized
Skills

Chapter 8

5-String Fundamentals

Even though Tony Levin says three is enough, the 5-string bass has earned a place in many players' arsenals. Normally tuned *BEADG*, the 5's increased range, additional positions, and expanded timbral variety open up possibilities unknown to 4-stringers. And as the 5-string's design has matured, it's becoming easier to jump into low-*B* land. Manufacturers have figured out how to make great-sounding 5-strings in almost every price range.

Tech Talk

Debuting in the mid '70s, the first 5-strings varied greatly in neck width. Some builders squeezed five strings into the space of four, while others kept standard P-Bass spacing all the way across. This extreme range made it difficult for hardware manufacturers to establish standards; many early 5-string bridges featured movable saddles to accommodate constantly changing specs. "About ten years ago my first 5-strings were Jazz Bass-style: 21 frets, 1¾" at the nut, 2⅞" at the last fret," recalls New York luthier Roger Sadowsky. "Players wanted 24 frets and wider spacing, so we went with 1⅞" at the nut and 3³⁄₁₆" at the 24th fret. With a 24-fret neck we had to move the pickups closer to the bridge to leave room for slapping, so we needed bigger-sounding pickups to compensate for the loss of bottom."

The 5's string spacing has now settled into two main varieties: The wider has 3/4" spacing at the bridge, which provides more room for slapping. The narrower has 5/8" spacing, which allows faster string crossing, makes chordal playing easier, and keeps the neck width narrower overall. In some basses the string spacing is narrow at the nut but flares out significantly toward the bridge, combining a more playable lower-fret feel with more room for slapping.

The biggest challenge is building a 5 with a good-sounding *B* string. To combat flabby *B* syndrome, some companies offer 35" and even 36" scales instead of the more common 34". But while the extra length bolsters the *B*, not all players are comfortable with the longer scale.

Another method of increasing B-string clarity is to run the strings through the body, which can add up to 1 1/2" of string length without changing the playing scale. Neck stability also affects *B*-string tone; a number of builders use graphite to add stiffness. Perhaps the most radical approach to B-string tension appears on the Dingwall Voodoo bass. Its Ralph Novak-designed fanned-fret fingerboard yields scale measurements from 34" on the *G* string to 37" on the *B*.

Of course, there are plenty of 34"-scale basses that achieve well-defined *B*'s through careful attention to body and neck woods, bridge density, string down-force at the bridge saddle, neck-joint solidity, and overall craftsmanship.

Strings

Strings play a major role in determining whether your axe has the crystal-clear lows of a Steinway grand or the murky overtones of a large steel drum. Indeed, the search for a better *B* has spurred big string-technology improvements in the past ten years. *B* gauges now range from .115 to a whopping .145, with .125 to .130 standard for 5-string sets. But, notes La Bella's Bob Archigian, "There's more to strings than the diameter. Different cores, windings, and tapering all can produce a different character."

Bassists remain sharply divided on whether a tapered *B* string sounds best. The narrower over-the-saddle gauge can make the tapered *B* easier to intonate and give it better sustain. But in BASS PLAYER's March '96 String Shootout, editors found they preferred the sound of conventional strings, perhaps because the increased mass at the bridge produces more body resonance. If you switch from conventional strings, make sure you raise your *B*-string saddle to compensate for the taper.

Searching for a *B* string that works with your bass can be expensive. Fortunately, many companies have done extensive research into which strings bring out the best in their basses, so check with your instrument's manufacturer for recommendations.

Let's Shop

When trying out 5-strings, listen closely to the lower notes' tone. Slap a few notes from low *B* to low *D*. Is the sound clear or muddy? Play all the way up the neck on the *B* string. Is the timbre consistent? Check string tension. Does the *B* feel tight, or does it flap when you lay into it? Check the neck. Does it feel too wide? A 5-string neck can increase hand strain, so comfort is important. It takes time to adjust to a 5-string's extra width, but sometimes you can tell right away if a particular 5 is going to work for you.

Neck contour also affects feel; a wide neck with a fat, round contour is too much for some players. There are lots of neck options, though, including asymmetrical profiles that put more wood under the *B* string than under the *G*.

Check the bass's sonic balance by playing across the strings. If you notice a marked drop in *B*-string volume, check the pickup's magnet placement by testing it with a ferrous object such as a paper clip. If the magnet doesn't extend far enough under the *B* string, the sound won't be balanced. Fortunately there are many choices available for 5-string pickups, with the J-Bass and "soapbar" styles well represented. If you find an axe has the right feel but a less-than-ideal sound, you may be able to improve it.

For more information about choosing a 5, see BASS PLAYER's January '97 Ultimate 5-String Shootout (**www.bassplayer.com/gear**).

Plugging In

When you finally get your 5-string, take it easy at first. Your hands need to adjust to the wider neck, and you'll likely feel additional stress about hitting wrong notes. On your initial gigs carry your 4 as a backup in case your hands, brain, and bandmates need a break.

One detail you must address is the need for additional muting. When playing the *A*, *D*, and *G* strings, free-ringing open *B* and *E* strings can be a problem. Start with your thumb on the pickup when playing the *B* and *E* strings. When you move across to the *A* string, dropping your thumb to the *B* will keep it quiet, and your upstroke will mute the *E* when your finger comes to rest against it. When switching to the *D* string, drop your thumb to the *E* and let it cover the *B* as well; this keeps these two muted. Playing the *G* string requires you to leave the thumb notched between the *B* and *E*—while you also use your 3rd finger to cover the *A* string. This takes some getting used to, but it's essential to developing clean right-hand technique. (Just be glad you're not playing a 6-string yet.)

Not having *E* as your lowest string requires mental adjustment, and it will be tempting to overuse the extra low notes. Sure, they sound great, but they also carry a lot of weight. The great 5-string players use the lower range sparingly, deliberately, and *musically*. Listen for *B*-string notes on recordings to learn how the best bassists employ them for emphasis and drama. Ex. 1 shows where those tones sit on the staff.

Ex. 1

One of the 5-string's biggest advantages is additional positions—you now have two places to play low *E* through low *A♭* (Fig. 1). This lets you stay in one position longer, make bigger jumps with less effort, and explore new timbral possibilities. Playing above the 5th fret on the *B* string—instead of stretching for notes on the *E*— also gives your arm and hand a break.

Fig. 1

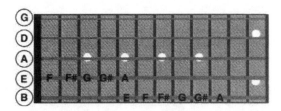

The first four times through Ex. 2, play the way you would on 4-string—using an open *E*—and then transfer that note to the *B* string's 5th fret for the last four times. The line will feel and sound different, with more depth and a darker timbre to the *E*. Ex. 3 shows how you can use the *B* string to play an extended *G* major scale in one position; Ex. 4 does the same (except for a final one-fret stretch) with diatonic 7th chords in *G*. Ex. 5 shows a simple arpeggiated bass line over a I–IV–V progression that uses all five strings in one position. Ex. 6 is a finger-funk line that drops to low *D* in the last bar for emphasis. It's also cool to lay into the low *B* string. Ex. 7 is a 3/4 slap line that emphasizes the low *D*. Slapping this low will give you a clear indication how good your *B* string really is.

As you work with your 5, more possibilities will reveal themselves, and you'll find that in many ways it's a different instrument than the 4. Once your hands adapt and your brain adjusts, you may discover you feel naked without your *B* string.

TRACK
33

Ex. 2

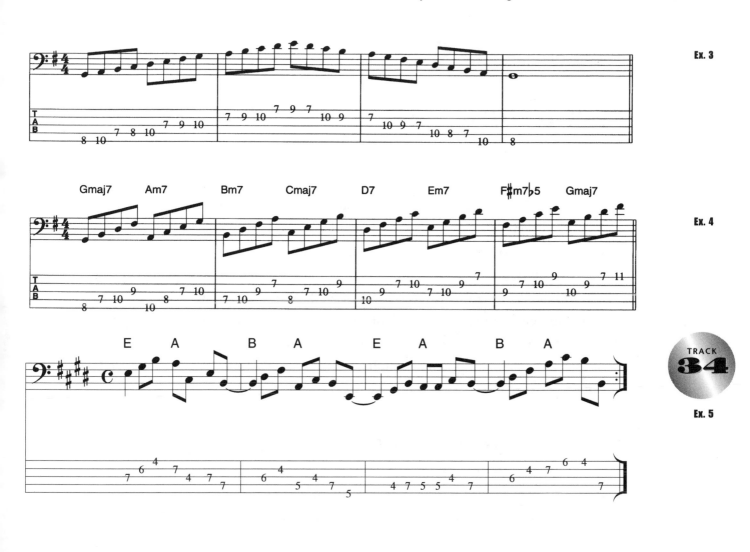

Ex. 3

Gmaj7 Am7   Bm7 Cmaj7   D7   Em7   F#m7♭5 Gmaj7

Ex. 4

E A   B A   E A   B A

TRACK **34**

Ex. 5

TRACK **35**

Ex. 6

T P T P T H P T H P T P T P T P P P T P T P T H P T H P T P T P T P

Ex. 7

Chapter 9

Doubling

When Leo Fender introduced the Precision Bass in 1951, he gave bassists a viable choice between electric and acoustic. Each instrument has its devotees. For decades, hard-core electrophiles have debated with acoustic purists over which instrument is the "real" bass. But many of us have chosen to sidestep this argument by playing both.

"Doubling" opens up two categories of work. You can take gigs on the other bass, and many gigs go exclusively to doublers. Plus, you gain the opportunity to express yourself in a wider range of musical situations, and you can learn the unique beauty of each bass. Here's information you'll need to become a doubler, coming from either direction.

Moving from Electric to Acoustic

Acoustic basses can be intimidating. They're big, expensive, sometimes hard to find, and have a 41" to 43" string lengths (with no frets), and they take years to master. Faced with those challenges, many electric bassists stick with what they know. But if the upright's challenges scare you away, you'll never know the joy of playing a booming low F and hearing the note swell and sustain for as long as you can keep your finger down. No fretless electric can match the growl of a well-set-up acoustic upright. Feeling the vibrations in the huge body, the subtleties of tone, and the pure acoustic sound of your hands working with the instrument is an incredible experience. Yes, it's a lot of work, and it requires dedication, patience, and some cash to get started—but your travails will be well rewarded the day you are good enough to gig on acoustic.

Finding a bass. First, you have to get an instrument. If you live near a major metropolitan area, you'll have more choices. Look in the Yellow Pages for stringed-instrument shops. You may find a bass in a regular music store; call around. Check the newspaper's used-instrument listings. Pawnshops are another option. And ask other bassists. If there is a symphony orchestra where you live, contact the bassists and see if they have anything for sale or know someone who does. There are several shops around the country that cater to acoustic bassists, stocking a good selection of instruments. Their inventory will be higher quality—and higher priced. There are also mail order houses that stock new factory-made basses, both plywood and carved. These instruments' quality can vary greatly. Inquire about the instrument's origin. Some brands have been around awhile and can be trusted, but a bass with a German-sounding name might come from Sri Lanka.

Be prepared to spend a minimum of $1,000 for a plywood bass. The days of finding an old Kay for $300 are gone—unless you are *really* lucky. A plywood bass is fine to start with; they are less expensive than carved instruments, and if set up well can sound excellent. Carved basses are pricier, more prone to cracking, and more expensive to maintain. If you luck into a decent carved bass for a reasonable price, go for it; you can always get your money back if you decide to sell it.

There are many crossover-style instruments on the market. Some of them approximate the feel of a real upright, while others are designed to help the electric player make an easy transition to upright-style playing with a shorter string length. While these basses have their merits, don't mistake them for the real thing. Someone who learns on a short-scale solidbody electric upright wouldn't last for one tune on a regular acoustic upright. If you think using one of these instruments will make you an upright player, think again.

If you have a friend who plays upright, bring him or her along to check out the instrument you're considering. Keep in mind it may need work, and it may be hard for you to tell if the bass is a diamond in the rough, or just rough. Some signs indicate major problems; others are less serious, requiring only routine repairs. (For more detailed information, read "How to Buy & Care for an Acoustic Bass" in the March '95 BASS PLAYER.)

Warning signs. When you first look at a bass, notice the string height. Are the strings a mile off the fingerboard? This could be simply a matter of setup. Check where the neck joins the body. Are there any signs of a repair job? A poorly refit neck joint can make an instrument very difficult to get into playing shape. If the job was done right, though, it won't affect playability. Look at the top, particularly around the bridge feet. Basses can develop dips or bumps if the soundpost has been too tight. Also look for soundpost-related cracks along the back. Examine the fingerboard—is there a lot of wood left on it, or has it been planed down to a sliver? Check the seam where the fingerboard is glued to the neck. Is it glued on straight and securely? Look down the fingerboard to see if there are high spots that need planing. Check for open seams by rapping along the edges of the bass with a knuckle. Seams are easy to fix—

but if they're open, you won't get a full sense of how the bass sounds. Finally, play the bass and check for rattles. The bass bar is an important component. It's a long wooden strip that is glued to the top under the *E* string bridge foot and runs the length of the top. The bass bar transmits vibrations to the top and gives the instrument stability. If it's loose, it may rattle or let the top sink in from the tension—and most certainly affect the sound. Repairing it means taking off the top, which can cost around $300. Make sure you have your friend play the bass, and listen to how it sounds from a variety of positions.

Strings. Once you've found something that's affordable and looks solid, most likely you'll need new strings. Upright strings are relatively expensive; do some research before you buy. First, determine what type of playing you'll do. There are strings that suit classical playing, but if you want to play jazz, you'll need strings that work well for pizzicato (plucking). Fortunately, many manufacturers label their strings accordingly. If you are into bluegrass or blues, you may want gut or nylon strings to get a more authentic sound. There are also newer strings that claim to be good all-around choices. (Bass Player's March '96 article "Searching for the Perfect Upright Strings" is an excellent source of information.

The bridge. Now that you have your strings, look at the bridge. Height adjusters—wheels that allow you to raise and lower the bridge—are very important. Does your bridge have them? When you first start out, you'll want to keep the strings lower to save your hands; there's no glory in wrestling a bass with 3" action when you're beginning. As you get stronger, you may want to raise the action to make the bass louder. If your bass doesn't have height adjusters, have them installed by a good acoustic-bass technician. If the wheels can be fitted to your existing bridge, it will cost $100 to $150. If you need to get a new bridge cut, it can run you between $200 and $300. (Of course, prices will vary.) If you can't find a good repairperson, be willing to travel—or take your chances with someone at a guitar shop. Once you get the strings on and lowered to a reasonable height, you may discover the fingerboard has some buzzes. Getting the fingerboard professionally "dressed" can make a huge difference in how a bass sounds and feels.

The bow. Did you remember to buy a bow? You soon-to-be upright jazzers will need one. It's the best way to tune the bass, and, most important, it's the most effective way to learn how to play in tune. Pizzicato playing allows a high margin of error; the bow, however, is a merciless microscope that will painfully pinpoint your intonation flaws. It may be hard to listen to at first, but deal with it. The pain will pay off later.

You have the choice between a French or German bow (Fig. 1). There are advantages to both: The French bow is held overhand, like a violin bow; it has the potential for better articulation and easier string crossing. The German bow is held underhand, giving you greater power and volume, and in my opinion is easier to learn. A good bow can cost more than a bass, but you can buy a fiberglass bow with real hair (not synthetic) for around $50. That's good enough for now.

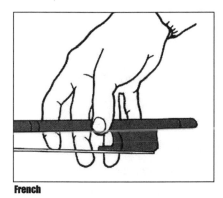
French

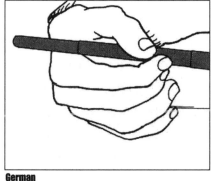
German

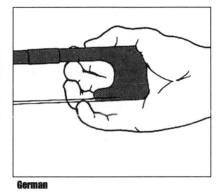
German

Fig.1

You'll need rosin for your bow—it's near impossible for the bow hair to grip the strings without it. Get rosin made specifically for bass; violin and cello rosin isn't sticky enough, Carlsson Swedish Bass Rosin and Pop's are two brands pro players favor. If you live in a warm climate make sure you keep the rosin in its plastic container in a cool place. Heat will make rosin soft and runny, and you may wind up with a formless blob the texture of thick honey.

Technique. At this point you'll need to find a teacher to help you progress faster and avoid technical pitfalls that could develop into physical problems. Upright bass is a physically demanding instrument, and an inefficient approach could set you back. Ask around for a referral to a teacher who plays the style you like—but make sure the teacher can teach you to use the bow. Someone who says you don't need to learn bowing is steering you down the road to bad intonation. Every teacher has preferences for books, but you should get into one of the time-tested classical methods. The three big names to look for are Nanny, Simandl, and Billè; these methods will help with scales, arpeggios, string crossing, and neck positions.

New acoustic players' most common technical mistake is using electric-bass technique. It's important to know the differences between one-finger-per-fret electric technique and traditional acoustic technique. Because of the upright's long string length and the extra hand strength required, most acoustic players mainly use only three fingerboard-hand fingers—the index, middle, and ring finger and pinkie together. This is called the Simandl method. If you start out trying to use one finger per semitone on an upright fingerboard, you're asking for physical problems in your hand and arm.

There are differences in plucking-hand technique, too. Your plucking fingers' pads won't be tough enough to withstand the torture an upright bass can dish out—you could end up with blisters that take weeks to heal. Use the side of your index finger from the middle knuckle down; the skin is tougher there, and you'll get a fatter sound. (For your public acoustic-upright debut, bring your electric bass. You may not have the stamina to last a whole night on upright.)

Playing out. Once you've been studying and practicing for a while, your hands will be stronger, you'll have applied some of your musical knowledge to the instrument, and you'll be ready to jam. First, think about what you're going to do. Are you playing with a bunch of acoustic guitars or a piano? No amp is needed. But add a drummer, and you need an amp. Otherwise, you won't be heard, and you'll burn out your hands trying. You've probably heard stories of the "good old days" when "real" bassists played seven-hour big band gigs without an amp and were heard just fine. Those days are gone. Drummers play louder, horn players use microphones, guitarist are always amplified, keyboards are often electric. If you want to use gut strings with super-high action only to be "felt" and not heard, be prepared to suffer.

Pickups & amps. There are many options for amplifying upright. Depending on how loud you need to be, you have the choice of a transducer pickup, a microphone, a combination (my preference), or—if you really have to crank it up—a magnetic pickup. (For more on these options, check out "Electric Wood: Acoustic Upright Amplification Basics" in the October '98 BASS PLAYER (**www.bassplayer.com/gear**). Many piezo pickups require a buffer preamp. That's because the piezo pickup's output impedance is hotter than most amps' input impedance, so the pickup "loads" the input, causing reduced low-frequency response. When buying a pickup, find out if it needs a preamp—most manufacturers make preamps that match their pickups.
Next you'll need an amp. Chances are your upright isn't going to sound good through your SVT. A small sealed cabinet works best for the upright; standing in front of a huge cab is an invitation to feedback, not to mention a woofy, indistinct sound. A 12" speaker is just fine for acoustic bass; a 15" works great, and some 2x10 cabinets work well, too. If you are trying to compete in a full-volume blues band, you may need to go through the PA. I've never had much luck with the upright at super-high volumes. It can be done, but don't let go of the strings for a second, or you'll hear the worst gut-rattling, speaker-blowing feedback of your life.

After a while, your hands will be strong, your intonation will be accurate, you'll learn how to get the right sound for the gig, and you'll feel a tremendous sense of accomplishment. And when word gets out that you play upright, your phone will be ringing with all sorts of new opportunities.

Upright Exercises

To get started on the bow, play long tones along with a metronome. Start with open strings to get a feel for your bowing hand (Ex. 1). Good tone requires learning to control bow speed and pressure on the strings. Each string responds differently; the *G* and *D* will speak without too much effort, but the *A* and *E* are a little harder to get moving. As you play closer to the bow's tip, you'll need to add a little pressure because your hand weight will be at its farthest from the string. Focus on smooth, consistent movement—picture your bow arm moving in a circle as you change from down bow (your arm moving away from your body) to up bow (your arm moving toward your body). See how refined you can make it sound—you don't want to saw the bass in half.

Ex. 1

Next, practice one-octave major scales. Follow the recommended fingerings; they are your key to good intonation. Ex. 2 shows fingerings for the most common major keys. Fingering numbers that are followed by a forward slash (/) indicate a shift to a higher position, and numbers followed by a backward slash (\) indicate a shift to a lower position. Pay attention to your sound. Are you close to being in tune? If you have a keyboard available, make a tape of the major scales to practice with (use a straight piano sound). Match your pitch with the keyboard's. Is your volume consistent? How is your tone? The acoustic bass requires you to become a good listener.

Ex. 2

Moving from Acoustic to Electric

First, rid yourself of any attitude of superiority, and approach the electric bass with dignity and humility. (If you think it's a toy, listen to Victor Wooten.) When you experience the sheer power of one open *E* whole-note played through a high-powered stack, you'll see what the instrument has in store.

Getting a bass. You're lucky—electric basses are easy to find and can be inexpensive. Just about every music store has a selection, and you can find good used deals. Be prepared to spend between $300 and $500 for a decent starter electric; you can find them for cheaper, but quality suffers in the low range. Ask around and try several models. I recommend starting out with a 4-string—it will feel more familiar than a 5 or 6. You may be tempted to go for a fretless. Sure, you'll be able to transfer *some* of your left-hand technique, but remember most electrics have a 34" scale length, as opposed to acoustic's 40"-plus. I suggest starting with a fretted bass.

Check the neck width at the nut. The narrow "Jazz" neck (named after the Fender Jazz Bass) is 1 1/2" at the nut, while the slightly wider "Precision" neck (named after the Fender Precision) is 1 3/4" at the nut. You'll also find 1⅝" necks. Try each.

Pickups. Electric basses also have a variety of pickup configurations (Fig. 2). The Jazz Bass setup consists of two single-coil pickups—one near the bridge and one near the fingerboard. This system is preferred for thumbstyle (slap-and-pop) and for jazz playing—the pickup placement gives you more highs and better articulation for faster playing. A disadvantage of this system is the hum that occurs when both pickup volumes aren't turned up full. Some basses have internal shielding to lessen this problem; you'll notice the difference when you're trying out different basses.

The Precision setup consists of one split pickup in the middle of the pickguard; this gives you a strong, punchy tone with a deep bottom and less highs. It's good for fat, round bass sounds, which work well in blues, rock, country, and reggae. Precision-type basses can be used for funk and jazz as well; it's a matter of preference. You will also see the "PJ" setup, which consists of a Precision-style pickup in front and a Jazz-style pickup at the bridge. This can offer a good compromise in the quest for big bottom and clear highs.

Many companies offer their own pickup designs. A common type is the "soapbar," named because of its rectangular shape. Different soapbars often look identical, though inside they might be P-style, J-style, or "humbucker." Humbucker pickups have two coils that cancel out each other's hum. They are quiet, generally louder, and tend to offer fewer high frequencies than single-coil pickups. There are also humbuckers that look like single-coil Jazz bass pickups, so ask to make sure you know what you're buying.

P-style   J-style   PJ-style

Fig. 2

Basses can be passive or active. Passive basses rely only on the strings and pickups to create the sound. Active basses have a built-in preamp circuit that can boost volume and tone. Some active setups allow you to boost or cut lows and highs, and some have an additional midrange control. These choices are a matter of taste. Some players like the active controls' flexibility, while other prefer passive basses' simplicity. Try out both—and remember, a passive bass can always be upgraded with an active tone circuit.

Amps. If you already have an upright-bass amp, you can use that to practice with or to play small gigs. Just remember: If you have something small like a Polytone Mini-Brute, there's only so much it can take; these amps are not designed to pump out heavy electric bass. When you get next to a drummer, you'll be pushing the amp and risking a blown speaker or circuit.

There are many good medium-size combo amps (amp and speaker in one enclosure). Look for something that has either a 15" speaker, two 10" speakers, or four 10" speakers, and a minimum of 200 watts. Low frequencies require lots of power, so the more you have, the cleaner your sound. Many new amp designs include a tweeter for reproducing the highs, which is good if you want to get into slap bass. Another option is to get a separate speaker cabinet and a "head"—a combined preamp and power amp. This setup has one big advantage: you can mix and match components for the best sound and convenience. If you're playing a small gig you can bring a

2x10 cab, and if it's a heavy rock gig you can bring a 1x15 plus a 4x10 for maximum volume. Combos are generally less expensive than separate head/cabinet systems, and they're easier to transport. Find something that suits your needs—and your checkbook.

Strings. Most electric bassists use roundwound strings; they sound brighter, which makes them better suited for funk and harder-edged rock. Roundwounds come in stainless-steel and nickel. Stainless-steel strings are brighter-sounding and last longer—but since the metal is harder, it increases fret wear. Nickel strings don't sound quite as bright and go dead sooner, but some people prefer their sound. The standard gauges are (*G* string to *E*): .045, .065, .085, .105. Some electric players use lighter-gauge strings, but the heavier standard gauge will likely feel better to you. Flatwound strings are making a comeback; they have a mellower sound, produce less string noise, and feel more familiar to upright players. Flatwounds can be a good choice if you don't intend to play slap-style.

Technique. Find a teacher. There are many fine points to electric bass playing, and you'll be able to deal with the technical and conceptual differences most effectively if you have someone to guide you. For instance, if you are a classical player making the switch, you'll have to learn a whole new approach to pizzicato. But if you do choose to go it alone, there are many good books and videos available.

Physically, making the transition from upright to electric is easier, because your hands are used to playing something much more difficult. Unfortunately, this can cause a problem: You may tend to overplay. While it may be fun to let your fingers fly, remember that you still have to be supportive; overplaying will not endear you to your fellow musicians. On upright, the string response is slower, because the strings are longer, and the sound goes through the bridge and the soundpost and gets dispersed throughout the top and back. By the time the note has fully formed, it has traveled some distance. Electric bass attack is much faster; when you play the note, it's *right there*. This means you'll have to adjust your sense of time a bit—otherwise, you may rush.

Electric's full, punchy sound takes up a lot of sonic space, so economy is extremely important. If you listen to Jaco Pastorius or James Jamerson, you will hear them playing a lot. However, pay attention to *how* they play—it's not just the number of notes, it's how and when they play them. To get a really good sense of how the electric bass works, listen to the many ways it gets used in a variety of styles.

Electric Exercises

To get used to electric bass's attack, set your metronome at a medium tempo and play steady eighth-notes (Ex. 3). A common approach to playing rock bass, this is also a good way to develop consistent tone, volume, and rhythm.

Ex. 3

There are three systems of electric bass fingering. The first uses one finger per fret (Ex. 4). This method gives you the left-hand flexibility to execute difficult passages. Never stretch your hand too much, though; use a slight pivot between your 2nd and 3rd fingers.

Ex. 4

The second method is similar to upright fingering (Ex. 5). For playing octaves and 5ths, use your 1st finger on the root and the 4th finger on the 5th and octave. This eliminates the hand stress caused by stretching across one or more strings. This is often called "box" fingering. In the lower positions, it may be easier to use the 1-2-4 fingering for half-steps.

Ex. 5

The third approach is extension fingering. By keeping the wrist low and the hand open, you can stretch across more frets and play whole-steps between the fingers 1-3-4 (Ex. 6). This can help you avoid the unwanted string noise position shifts cause. It also opens up new musical opportunities—just make sure you don't strain your left hand. Just as you do with acoustic bass, always warm up on electric—slow scales work well.

Gig Tips

If you have to double on a gig, consider bringing two amps. I have yet to find a rig that sounds equally good for electric and acoustic; the sonic requirements are too different. For upright you need a tight, focused sound with the EQ voiced for piezo pickups. Electric bass needs lots of power and a speaker cabinet that moves some air. For doubling gigs I bring a small but effective electric rig: a 300-watt head and a ported 2x10 cabinet. I put my little acoustic-bass combo on top of that. It's a lot to carry— but if you want to sound your best on both instruments, you need to have the right equipment. Some people have success playing upright and electric through a small 2x10 cabinet with separate preamps. Bear in mind, though, that an amp designed for electric bass may not have the best EQ for upright. There's another disadvantage to running both basses through the same rig: when you switch instruments, you will definitely need to change your EQ and volume settings. This takes time, and you may not get the settings right. Having a dedicated amp for each allows you to dial in the sound and leave it, allowing for smoother transitions. If you do run both basses into the same amp, use an A/B switching device so you don't have to do any unplugging.

Make sure you have enough room to safely put down your acoustic bass; you may have to make a quick transition, and you don't want to damage it. If you can, find a corner to stand the upright in. Remember to protect the bridge; a slight knock can ruin your setup. You may want to invest in an acoustic stand. Have a stand for your electric bass as well, and keep your cords arranged neatly.

If your band uses a set list, talk to the leader about programming the set for minimal bass changes—switching every other tune is a big hassle. If you are playing in a

▪ Double Talk ▪

Here's what three well-known doublers have to say about playing both acoustic and electric bass.

John Patitucci

For the last several years I've gotten back into my classical playing, and it's helped my overall playing a lot. Switching back and forth is tricky; my way has always been just to play both a lot. I've had to keep my mind open enough to switch back and forth, because a lot of it is mental.

It's always been a little juggling act for me to keep them both going. With my workload now, it's not always possible to play both basses every day, but recently I started getting up early every morning and practicing for an hour with the bow. One of the big differences between the electric and acoustic has to do with the left hand. On the electric, we're always striving for total independence of each finger, except down low, where I use the 1st and 4th fingers for whole-steps. On acoustic, if you play the traditional way, the 1st and 2nd fingers are independent, with the 3rd and 4th always together.

Bunny Brunel

I started on the acoustic, but only a week later I started doubling on the electric bass. In fact, one of the reasons I got the gig with Chick Corea in 1978 was because I could play all of the electric bass material from *Return to Forever* [ECM] as well as the acoustic bass work from *Friends* [Polydor]. The electric bass helped me figure out where the notes are on the acoustic. To maintain a high level of performance on the two instruments, you just have to practice both all of the time. I use electric bass technique on both instruments [using all four fingers, even in the 1st position].

Reggie Hamilton

I've always felt they are two different instruments, and there were just as many challenges on electric as on acoustic. They both require a lot of attention. On electric you need to practice harmonics, scales, slapping, and playing with the pick. On upright, someone may ask you to sound like Jimmy Blanton, Oscar Pettiford, or Tommy Potter. You need to know both instruments' history. As far as bowing is concerned, practice, practice, practice—there are no two ways about it. If you practice with the bow all the time, your pizzicato intonation will just get better.

On show gigs where I'm doubling I don't always have time to make the segue, so I just sling my electric behind my back and pick up the upright—I have strap locks on all my electrics.

pit orchestra, you may have to change frequently. A good arranger knows it takes a while to switch basses and will write in enough time for you to make the transition. In a fast-paced variety show, you may have to change instruments quickly. With cramped quarters and an inefficient setup, switching basses can be a real challenge, so check the music and see where your switches are. If necessary, practice your transitions with a metronome clicking the tempo and see if you have enough time—you can't afford to miss your cue. Use your A/B switch or a volume pedal to make switches quietly.

■ Resources ■

Here are some books on core skills and different styles for electric and upright; **www.bassbooks.com** and **www.lemurmusic.com** are good online sources.

Electric

Bass Essentials, Bunny Brunel [Mel Bay]

Bass Fitness, Josquin Des Pres [Hal Leonard]

Funk Bass, Jon Liebman [Hal Leonard]

Funkifying the Clave: Afro-Cuban Grooves for Bass, Lincoln Goines & Robbie Ameen [Warner Bros.]

The Funkmasters: The Great James Brown Rhythm Sections, Dr. Licks & Chuck Silverman [Warner Bros.]

Reggae Bass, Ed Friedland [Hal Leonard]

Standing in the Shadows of Motown: The Life & Music of Legendary Bassist James Jamerson, Dr. Licks [Hal Leonard]

The True Cuban Bass, Carlos D'l Puerto & Silvio Vergara [Sher]

Upright

The Evolving Bassist Millennium Edition, Rufus Reid [Myriad]

Jazz Bass; Building Walking Bass Lines; Expanding Walking Bass Lines; Bass Improvisation; Ed Friedland [Hal Leonard]

Melodic Playing in the Thumb Position, Michael Moore [Advance]

Methode Complete pour la Contrebasse, Edouard Nanny [Leduc]

New Method for Double Bass, T. Simandl [Carl Fischer]

Nuovo Metodo per Contrabbasso, Isaia Billè [G. Ricordi]

The instruments' physical differences cease to be an obstacle once you've spent some time with both. Until that happens, stay as relaxed as possible. Remember to make the micro-adjustments in your right-hand attack so you don't rush or drag. Doubling will improve your playing on your primary bass, and you'll find ways to incorporate your new musical perspectives and open up new paths of expression.

Chapter 10

The Thumb Thing: How to Get an Upright Sound on Electric Bass

These days when somebody mentions playing with the thumb, the first thing that comes to mind is slapping. But don't forget that the bass guitar was originally designed to be plucked with a downward thumb motion. Ever notice the finger rest below the *G* string on P-Basses? It's there so you can rest your index, middle, and ring fingers while you play with your thumb. To keep the strings from ringing when they weren't supposed to, Fender glued a foam strip to the underside of the bridge cover (a favorite ashtray for '70s bassists). This muted the strings, resulting in a short note-decay time that approximated upright bass sound.

In Dr. Licks' James Jamerson tribute *Standing in the Shadows of Motown: The Life & Music of Legendary Bassist James Jamerson* [Hal Leonard], look at the photos of the artists who played on the accompanying CD. You'll see some of them shoved foam strips under their strings at the bridge to help them simulate the old Motown sound. (Jamerson used the original bridge-plate mute and flatwound strings.) After the book came out, players started sticking foam under their strings in an attempt to get Jamerson's sound. (If only it were that simple!) This makes an effective mute—but getting a piece of foam in and out between tunes can be a problem. You can achieve similar results by muting the strings with your right-hand palm. This technique creates some different articulation possibilities, giving you greater control over your sound. Thumb-and-mute is one of the most useful techniques I have—and on some gigs, it's the only way I play.

The right-hand muting technique helps you simulate several styles:

- The upright-bass sound from early jazz, R&B, country, and rock & roll records. (Most of this article will deal with this application.)

- Certain synth-bass sounds you hear on modern R&B and rap records.
- The deep bass sound of salsa and reggae.

In addition, in some rooms it's the only way to get a decent sound. In very boomy halls, a sustained note fills up so much space it's impossible to hear or feel what you're playing. Muting keeps the notes short and gives you a nice, solid attack. And it sure beats cutting the lows and boosting the mids!

How To Do It

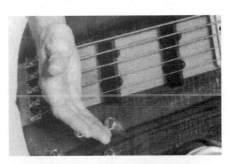

Fig. 1

The first step is to rest the side of your right hand on the strings just in front of the bridge (Fig. 1). Next, flatten out the hand so you can pluck the strings with your thumb with a downstroke (Fig. 2). This is the most common technique for walking quarter-notes; play Ex. 1 with your thumb, keeping the side of your hand against the strings close to the bridge. Each bass responds differently, so experiment with varying degrees of pressure on the strings.

Fig. 2

If you play a 5- or 6-string bass, you can get an even fatter sound by using the *B* string and playing higher on the neck (Fig. 3)—you knew those notes would come in handy one day! The heavier string gets even closer to the sound you want—plus, you'll get more familiar with the territory in those higher positions.

Fig. 3

The most common upright plucking technique is to use the side of the index finger to dig in, producing a full, meaty sound. After each note, you must reposition the index finger for the next attack; this creates a characteristic upright bass articulation on eighth-notes and triplets. The thumb downstroke technique is the perfect way to match this articulation on electric.

One advantage of right-hand muting vs. the foam mute is more control over note decay: The more pressure you put on the strings, the shorter the notes. On the other hand, the foam mute allows greater rhythmic articulation; you can play more-com-

Fig. 4

Fig. 5

Fig. 6

plex lines because your plucking-hand fingers can work in the usual manner. However, you do have some options with right-hand muting. For instance, you can use the thumb and index finger together. The thumb technique remains the same—downstrokes only—but you add the index finger to play additional notes with upstrokes (Fig. 4). This thumb-and-index technique works well when playing eighth-notes or triplets (Ex. 2).

Another approach uses only the index finger—not the thumb—in an upstroke motion (Fig. 5). This technique works for adding triplet "rakes" across three strings (Ex. 3). To get the classic rockabilly sound, put your thumb under the string a little and pull up slightly; the string will slap against the fingerboard, creating a slight click with each note. Practice playing Ex. 4 like this, and when Elvis comes out of hiding, you'll be ready for the gig!

Taking this idea a step further, you can add a muted thumb slap between each note, which simulates the acoustic slap-bass sound used in country, rockabilly, bluegrass, and early jazz (Fig. 6.) Ex. 5 puts this technique to good use.

TRACK **38**

Ex. 4

TRACK **39**

Ex. 5

Thinking Upright

Beyond sound, the most important aspect of the thumb-and-mute technique is learning how to think like an upright player. If you already play acoustic bass, you have an obvious advantage—but even so, there are many styles of upright playing. Right-hand muting techniques work extremely well for swing-era music as well as early rock, R&B, and country & Western—essentially, all styles of upright playing before the use of steel strings and the fast two-finger articulation Scott LaFaro pioneered.

Learn to choose your notes as an upright player would. You're not only thinking about playing a different instrument—you're thinking about playing in a different time period. Remember upright is physically much harder to play than the electric. This was particularly true in the days before amps and steel strings, when the action had to be set high to get the sound to project. The effort required to produce each note forced bassists to play deliberately and simply.

Rather than being outmoded, this concept makes sense for all bass styles. Because the electric is physically so much easier to play, bassists feel compelled to play more notes than necessary, simply because it's both easy and gratifying. To simulate that old upright bass style, you must strip down your lines to essentials. You have to play the line that's most obvious—and stick with it.

For most applications, if you play the right notes the thumb-and-mute technique works better than upright. As we discussed in the previous chapter, it can be tricky to amplify the acoustic bass. And unless you dedicate an upright to old-style setup, with gut strings and high action, you can't get it to sound the way people expect for swing and jump blues. For those kinds of gigs people usually expect me to bring my upright, but I bring my electric instead and use the thumb-and-mute technique. The sound is exactly what they want to hear, and I never get any complaints.

Swing-Blues Lines

For swing-style 12-bar blues, Ex. 6 is the line you'll use most. It's nothing new, but if you make it groove, it can be the best thing you could possibly play. This line is the basis for most swing, blues, Western swing, early rock & roll, and boogie-woogie. Listen to old Chuck Berry recordings, and the next time you play "Johnny B. Goode," skip the eighth-notes and play this walking line. Joey Spampinato, NRBQ's great bassist, uses lines like this quite often; for a good taste of his playing, check out the Chuck Berry documentary film *Hail! Hail! Rock 'n' Roll.*

In a line like this the space *between* the pitches is essential. In other words, pay attention to note length. When he wrote about Western swing in his BASS PLAYER column, Nashville session great David Hungate aptly noted the "more traditional, percussive swing feel" has "some air between the notes."

Another way to give Ex. 6 more of an upright feel is to use only the index finger of your left hand. To take it a step further, stay on one string as much as possible. Swing players tended to walk up and down the same string; many early upright bassists started on washtub bass, and this had a big effect on how they approached the upright.

It's possible to get away from Ex. 6 and still sound authentic—just try to keep your line obvious, goal oriented, and authoritative. Ex. 7 shows another way to play over the same blues progression. Notice the repeated notes. Until the 1930s, bassists played mostly in a two feel, using only half-notes; when the swing era began, playing quarter-notes in four became standard—but the early bassists would often just repeat notes, essentially doubling up the two feel. As jazz progressed, the walking bass line developed more melodic complexity.

Ex. 6

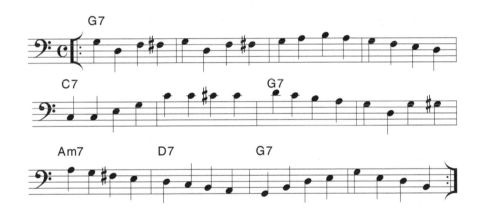

Ex. 7

Latin, Rap & Reggae

The thumb-and-mute technique works great in Latin music. For Ex. 8, go for the Ampeg Baby Bass sound.

Ex. 8

For synth-bass sounds, use the thumb and forefinger technique to play the eighth- and 16th-notes in Ex. 9. You can get different tones by palm pressure to control note decay.

TRACK **43**

Ex. 9

For reggae's huge, fat bass sound, palm muting acts as a lowpass filter, giving you a perceived bass-frequency boost. Try Ex. 10 on your next Bob Marley set.

Right-hand muting can be a great addition to your sonic arsenal. It dramatically changes your tone without expensive devices, and when used skillfully can create the perfect sound for many situations. In addition to practicing this chapter's techniques and learning to use the new sounds, listen to recordings to get into the concepts. Soon you'll be able to pass the blindfold test: Is it upright…or is it the thumb thing?

TRACK **44**

Ex. 10

If you've got the sound and your band still isn't happy, give them "the look" too.

Chapter 11

Bass Chords

Photographs by Jean Hangarter

Why play chords on the electric bass? Aren't we supposed to just lay down the groove and support our fellow musicians in a subtle yet authoritative manner?

Of course we are—but don't forget we're playing bass *guitar*. Chords are a legitimate weapon in our musical arsenal. And, from a practical standpoint, learning to play chord voicings helps you develop harmonic awareness. Unless you also play a chordal instrument, you can be at a disadvantage when it comes to knowing what happens above the root. Playing chords will teach you the structures of different chord types and—equally important—help you learn to hear them.

To start out, we'll cover the most basic chord forms: three-note voicings that consist of the root, 3rd, and 7th. The 3rd and the 7th are also called *guide tones*; the 3rd determines whether a chord is major or minor, and the 7th is the major scale's natural 7th or a flatted 7th. Different guide-tone combinations create the chord voicings we'll use.

There are two basic shapes for each of these voicings. One shape has the root on the *E* string, the other has the root on the *A* string. Due to the bass's low register, these voicings generally sound best when played above the 10th fret. The voicings with the root on the *E* string will skip over the *A* string entirely.

Left-hand tips. To get all three notes to sound together, you need to bend your first and second knuckles and arch your fingers (Fig. 1). Play on the tips of your fingers rather than the pads. Your fingertips may get a little sore at first, but you'll soon develop the calluses you need.

Fig. 1

The author demonstrating proper chord-playing position. Keeping the bass high helps you get the correct left-hand angle. (Ed's custom bass was built by Wolf Ginandes of the Musical Instrument Service Center in Boston; 617-247-0525.)

Right-hand position.
Playing closer to the bridge will help define each note's sound. To make the chords sound clear use only the bridge pickup, or use your tone controls to roll off low end.

Fig. 2

Right-hand tips. The cleanest right-hand approach is to use the thumb, index, and second fingers in a typical fingerpicking shape (Fig. 2). This lets you attack all three notes at the same time. Practice this technique and focus on making all the notes sound evenly balanced. You can also practice different fingerpicking combinations, such as thumb/1/2, thumb/2/1, 1/thumb/2, etc. Using all of these methods will help you develop a way to play chords and melody simultaneously.

Ex. 1 (with Charts 1–8) show six of the most common chord types, each built on an *A* root. Each chord is shown two ways: first with the root on the *E* string and then with the root on the *A* string. Ex. 2 (Charts 9–12) need all four notes to represent their true qualities, but we are using three-note voicings to make them playable. As a result, these "incomplete" voicings can double as other chords: the *Adim7* can also

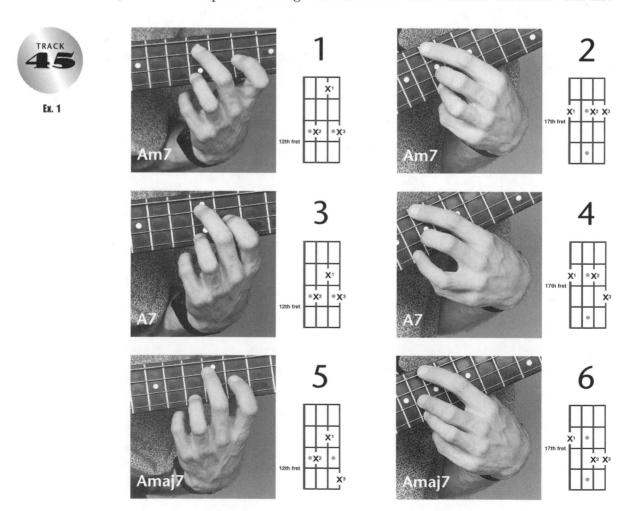

TRACK **45**

Ex. 1

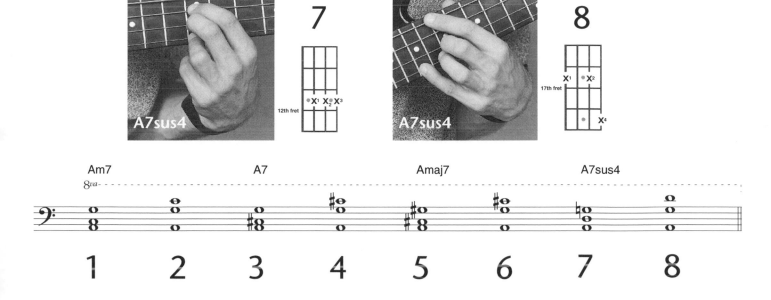

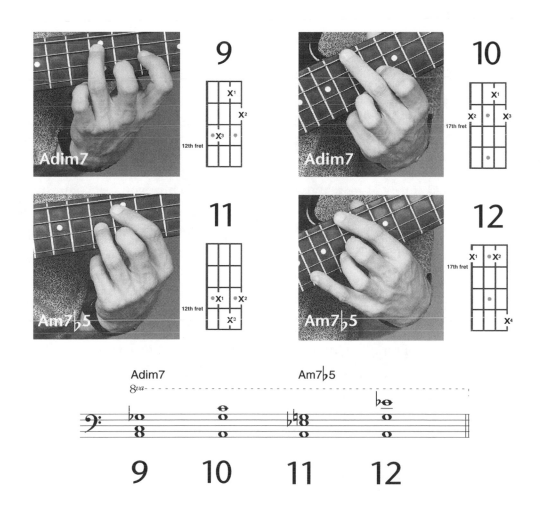

be used for *Am6*, and the *Am7♭5* can be used for *A7#11*. Practice these chords and listen carefully to the sounds different chord types and voicings make. (Notice that the notes are marked *8va*, which means they are played one octave higher than written.)

These are the basic voicings of the most common chord types. Once they feel comfortable under your fingers, practice switching from one to the other. Turn your metronome or drum machine to a slow tempo and play each voicing for two beats before moving on to the next one.

Here's a helpful hint for switching chords: Notice that most of these voicings have the 3rd finger on the *G* string. When switching chords, use this finger as an anchor. You may have to move only the 1st and 2nd fingers to get to the next voicing. This will prove to be handy as you tackle Ex. 3, a common jazz chord progression. All the voicings are taken from the 12 shapes you've just learned, but you will now play some of them on different roots—which requires moving around. Remember to use your 3rd finger as an anchor—let it be a "sliding guide" for your left hand as you move through the progression. (The numbers under each chord are the fingerings.)

TRACK **46**

Ex. 3

Play Ex. 3 slowly at first, and use *the metronome!* Once you feel comfortable with the mechanics of switching chords, pay attention to your sound. Try to balance each note so the chords sound clean and crisp. If your bass has two pickups, try using only the bridge pickup; this should make the chords sound less muddy. Picking close to the bridge will also clean up the sound. A little reverb is nice, too. On the CD I play through this progression six times; the first two passes are simply the chords in half-notes, as written. On the third and fourth pass I play them with a (hopefully) swinging rhythmic feel for more interest. The last two times I break up some of the chords with the right hand, and pick out some close-by melody notes to make it even more interesting. See what kind of variations you can find on your own.

5-string chords. The 5-string lets you find low notes above the 12th fret on the *B* string. These positions allow you to create chord voicings with a bigger spread between the root and guide tones. Ex. 4 shows you four new voicings with the root on the *B* string and the guide tones on the *D* and *G* strings. Because of the low register, we avoid using guide tones on the *A* and *E* strings.

When you have a chord with the root on the *E* string, you can find its lower 5th in the same fret on the *B* string. This lets you play chord patterns with alternating bass lines, a technique that works great for bossa nova. Ex. 5 is a bossa nova pattern with alternating bass.

Have fun with these voicings. They'll help you understand harmony and how it relates to the fingerboard, open up new doors to creative expression, annoy piano and guitar players by taking up their sonic space, and, of course, make you play three times better because you can now play three notes at a time instead of just one! Seriously, though—once you learn these chords well enough to take them out of the practice room, be careful how you apply them. They work great for solos, for backing up a melody line (try playing through a bossa nova with just sax, bass, and drums), or in a brave-new-world/go-for-the-throat venture like Primus. Just don't forget you still have to take care of business as a bass player.

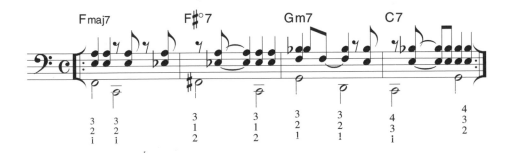

Ex. 4

Ex. 5

On the CD

Track 1: Tuning note *G*

Chapter 2: Navigating a Chord Chart

Track 2: Ex. 2, typical chord chart

Chapter 3: Training Your Ears

Track 3: Ex. 2, diatonic intervals

Track 4: Ex. 3, major modes

Track 5: Ex. 4, diatonic arpeggios

Track 6: Ex. 5, chromatic intervals

Track 7: Ex. 6, *F* natural minor

Track 8: Ex. 7, melodic minor

Track 9: Ex. 8, melodic minor modes

Track 10: Ex. 9, melodic minor arpeggios

Track 11: Ex. 10, harmonic minor

Track 12: Ex. 11, harmonic minor modes

Track 13: Ex. 12, harmonic minor arpeggios

Track 14: Single-note dictation

Track 15: Two-note dictation

Track 16: Three-note dictation

Track 17: Four-note dictation

Track 18: Diad dictation

Track 19: Triad dictation

Track 20: 7th-chord dictation

Track 21: Triads, first inversion

Track 22: Triads, second inversion

Track 23: Triads, mixed inversions

Track 24: 7th-chord inversions

Track 25: Two-chord progressions

Track 26: Four-chord progressions

Chapter 4: Faking It

Track 27: Ex. 1, root motion

Track 28: Ex. 3, dominant resolutions

Track 29: Ex. 4, II-V-I

Track 30: Ex. 5, modulations

Chapter 5: Puttin' on the Tux

Track 31: Random modulations

Chapter 7: Freelancing

Track 32: Ex. 3, Style-O-Rama

Chapter 8: 5-String Fundamentals

Track 33: Ex. 2, *E* lick on 4-string & 5-string

Track 34: Ex. 5, I-IV-V line

Track 35: Ex. 6, *D* funk lick

Track 36: Ex. 7, slap line

Chapter 10: The Thumb Thing

Track 37: Examples 1, 2, 3, basic lines

Track 38: Ex. 4, rockabilly blues in *G*

Track 39: Ex. 5, slap blues in *G*

Track 40: Ex. 6, swing blues in *G*

Track 41: Ex. 7, alternate *G* blues

Track 42: Ex. 8, salsa

Track 43: Ex. 9, rap, R&B

Track 44: Ex. 10, reggae

Chapter 11: Bass Chords

Track 45: Ex. 1, basic chords; Ex. 2, *Adim7, Am7♭5*

Track 46: Ex. 3, chord progression

Track 47: Ex. 4, 5-string chords

Track 48: Ex. 5, 5-string bossa

When It Comes to the Bass, We Wrote the Book.

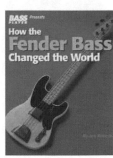